COACHING
RUGBY SEVENS
2ND EDITION

MARCUS BLACKBURN

BLOOMSBURY

LONDON • NEW DELHI • NEW YORK • SYDNEY

For my boys, Jack and Rory

Note

While every effort has been made to ensure that the content of this book is as technically accurate and as sound as possible, neither the author nor the publishers can accept responsibility for any injury or loss sustained as a result of the use of this material.

Published by Bloomsbury Publishing Plc
50 Bedford Square
London WC1B 3DP
www.bloomsbury.com

First edition 2006
Second edition 2013

ISBN (print): 978-1-4081-9213-9
ISBN (ePdf): 978-1-4081-9214-6
ISBN (ePub): 978-1-4081-0836-9

Acknowledgements
Cover photographs © Pavel L Photo and Video/Shutterstock.com (top left); © Kin Cheung/AP/Press Association Images (top right); © Julie Jacobson/AP/Press Association Images (bottom)
Inside photographs © see acknowledgements on page 156
Illustrations composed from cut-outs by David Gardner

Commissioned by Charlotte Croft

This book is produced using paper that is made from wood grown in managed, sustainable forests. It is natural, renewable and recyclable. The logging and manufacturing processes conform to the environmental regulations of the country of origin.

Typeset in 10pt on 15pt Myriad Pro by Margaret Brain, Wisbech, Cambs

Printed and bound in China by C&C Offset Printing Co.

10 9 8 7 6 5 4 3 2 1

CONTENTS

FOREWORD

The game of rugby is at an exciting stage. As I write this there are 100 countries included in the official International Rugby Board world rankings for the 15-a-side version of the game. The most significant development in recent years, however, is the growth of the seven-a-side game, for both male and female participants. This has been boosted by an incredibly popular and high quality world series of competitions and the inclusion of sevens as an Olympic sport.

Throughout the rugby world there are literally hundreds of coaching manuals and books that provide advice for players and coaches. Nearly all of them focus on the 15-a-side game. What is becoming obvious as time passes is that the skill set and tactics for the 15-a-side game do not apply to the seven-a-side version. There is a relative ignorance of the tactics and specialist sevens practice schedules in the majority of clubs and unions. Until now a potential sevens player or coach has little choice of useful reference material to turn to for assistance.

Marcus has enjoyed a close relationship with sevens both as a player and a coach. It is clearly his favourite version of the game. Although, like many of us, much of his time is taken up coaching the fifteen-a-side version of rugby, he has continued to follow and coach sevens when the opportunity arises. This has enabled him to refine and clarify his thinking and to be acutely aware of the difference between the 15-a-side and the sevens versions of the game.

This second edition of his book has been extensively revised in both organisation and contents, and provides an easy-to-understand guide for the preparation of players. Marcus's thoughts are clearly presented and supported with easy-to-follow diagrams. Tactical options are clearly distinguished from practice activities, all of which are designed to develop the skill and decision-making applicable to the game. The book offers an enhanced understanding of the sevens game and provides a squad with both theory and practice to make it competitive.

I believe that the book is a groundbreaking and effective addition to the family of rugby coaching manuals, and contains useful advice that is relevant for both players and coaches at all levels.

Brian O'Shea
July 2013

INTRODUCTION

Congratulations! You have just taken a huge step towards producing better rugby players – and not just for the sevens field. As you will have discovered, there are few coaching resources for the game of rugby sevens. This book does not just aim to fill the void, but to extend and accelerate education on the game, for coaches and players. The IRB's Laws of the Game should be referred to alongside the book, not only to promote up-to-date knowledge of the laws, but also to importantly connect readers with the world governing body for the game of Rugby Union.

On a tactical level, there is no bigger consideration than the number of players on the field. If you watch rugby sevens for long enough, a game of fifteens looks like it is being played on a postage stamp! Picture seven players spread out across the full width of a rugby field, and you will also picture the vast amount space available. Space is the number one principle of the game, and should be the biggest consideration in coaching rugby sevens.

From a technical perspective, it could be argued that the width of the pass is the key distinctive of sevens over fifteens, considering that most passes in sevens are longer than most passes in fifteens, and the inability to make long passes can certainly inhibit the use of space. However, an interesting statistic from a recent game between two top nations questions the value of passing in the game. Fiji beat Samoa by 19 points to 7, in a game when Samoa completed 69 passes and Fiji completed only 8! We can learn a lot from this, and unsurprisingly from Fiji in general.

Firstly, on possession. It has been asserted a countless number of times that possession is the key to the game. Sure, you have to have the ball to score, but Fiji teaches us that *purposeful* and *productive* possession is actually the key to success. Their alignment facilitated this, and gave them a framework to exploit their talents. Specifically, they

demonstrated how a deliberate and *spread* alignment can expand and stretch the defence to create space to run.

There is no doubt that the Fijian players had superlative running skills to break the Samoan defence, and outstanding defensive qualities to contain the Samoan attack. In this regard, sevens should be recognised as a game that requires, and develops, players with a complete skill set – players who are less specialist in terms of their position, who can attack *and* defend, can secure ball in contact, make decisions under pressure and communicate under fatigue. And then be fit enough to show repeat-efforts in all of the above. The game should *not* be viewed as an abbreviated form of rugby; rather, that it is rugby *magnified*. It is a closer inspection of the overall skills of rugby. Due to the increased exposure to a one-on-one situation, sevens enforces player accountability and promotes technical accuracy and, through this, provides a brilliant education for rugby players.

We may not all be fortunate enough to have superstars on our side who can change the game with a step or astound with sheer pace and flair, as Fiji did, but as a coach you should still be ambitious about producing a successful sevens team. What comes naturally to some can be developed through great coaching. Break down the action, and build up the players (*not* vice versa!). As coaches, we play an influential role in helping players to develop good habits in the game. This is done through repetition and raising awareness, guiding players to recognise opportunities and identify threats, before and as they happen. We should teach players what to look for, specifically related to space and numbers. This can be as simple as knowing who is marking you in attack, and whom you are marking in defence. It sounds like common sense, as all good coaching should, but still needs to be developed to become instinct in play. Practice does not make perfect, it makes *permanent*.

The first edition of *Coaching Rugby Sevens* presented a team structure and some innovative attacking movement patterns. Both made teams more organised and helped control possession. This second edition advances both the team structure and attacking movement patterns, enhanced by further analysis, development and revelation on the field. The book is no random or exhaustive collection of ideas, tactics and drills, but more a curriculum on the game, and a method for coaching it. The book aims to help players develop a toolbox of ideas that they can refer to in every situation on the field. Importantly, the lessons presented in each chapter should be viewed as a continuum; skipping lessons will only leave holes in your players' skill sets and in your own understanding of the game.

In this second edition of *Coaching Rugby Sevens*, theory and practice are entwined throughout the book, to facilitate the transfer of ideas. Lesson 8 demonstrates how to put all of the ideas together into a coaching programme, and encourages coaching through the game as the best method. A *whole-part-whole* approach is fitting and, by definition, promotes working on the 'whole' at least twice as much as working on the 'part'. Coaching through the game requires practice, but it is undoubtedly the best way to coach sevens, and the most efficient way to ensure transfer of skills and understanding from training to tournament.

The game of sevens is entertainment in itself and, in coaching it, you should not feel the need to entertain. There is no need for a wide variety of drills and practices, just ones that most effectively help the players understand the principles and acquire the necessary skills. There are 16 practical activities presented in this book (*see* pages 128–143), and all stay true to the fundamental shape of the game. There is little point in drills that set players running and passing in all directions, just for variety, as this does not happen in the game, and therefore should have no place in training. Stick close to the game; change dimensions and adjust numbers, but do not veer from the idea that sevens is a simple invasion game of running forwards and passing backwards, against defenders, to score tries.

As a new Olympic sport, rugby sevens has some catching up to do with those more established Olympic sports that have well-resourced high-performance programmes all over the world. Some countries, mainly those involved in the IRB Sevens World Series, are already there with world class programmes, but others still need to build the comprehensive pathways that lead to the elite level. Once in place, these initiatives will certainly create a pipeline for talent, but it is the quality of coaching that will ultimately determine the rate of improvement and overall standard of play in domestic, international and Olympic competition.

The very nature of the game of sevens, and the comparatively limited resources it requires, means that smaller nations can compete with the so-called rugby superpowers. My interest is to share an advanced understanding of the game

> The women's game is at a particularly exciting stage of development. The book aims to assist in the fast-tracking of female coaches and the overall advancement of the women's game, and it is for convenience only that it is written with masculine reference.

and proven coaching methods to raise the standard of play at all levels, to even the playing field for the Davids against the Goliaths, and to offer a curriculum for overall education on the game. There is no doubting the importance of fitness for sevens, and a conditioning guide to the game is available at www.marcusblackburn.com, but where athleticism is equal, the team with the best understanding will win. This book focuses on developing this understanding, and promotes brains for games!

By learning the lessons in each chapter and taking these ideas on to the training field, whether the players run the patterns perfectly or not, you are going to produce better rugby players, for your school, club or country, for sevens and fifteens. All players will have a better appreciation of space, more purposeful alignment, improved timing in their execution of skill, quicker anticipation in support, and better effort overall in attack and defence. Lesson 9 looks at how the key considerations of coaching sevens can influence how we coach and find success in fifteens. It promotes a new way of looking at the game, and presents some thought-provoking ideas to give power back to the attacking team, in an age when structured defences have prevailed. These ideas were notably borne on the sevens field. To keep in touch with how the game continues to advance, please contact me through www.coachingrugbysevens.com.

1

SEVENS IS A NUMBERS GAME

Attack in sevens is not rocket science, but it does involve simple mathematics. It is essential that players acknowledge the importance of *numbers* on the sevens field, and understand how an awareness of numbers, developed just by counting players, can have such a profound effect on achieving success in the game.

We are not talking about big numbers here – you never need to count up to more than seven. Sevens is an inclusive game, for all ages!

'Numbers!'

The worst-case scenario in attack is that you are faced with a 7 v 7 situation. The reality is that, in most cases, it will actually be 7 v 6, as most defences will choose to play with a sweeper behind the defensive line to cover kicks and line breaks. The effect that this simple numerical advantage has on the defence is a crucial consideration in attack, and underpins our ability to manipulate defenders. 'Numbers' is one of the most fundamental attacking options in the game, and is a simple call to signal that the defence is stretched and outnumbered on one side of the field. Players therefore have to develop the ability to exploit the overlap for the short time that it exists.

The problem is, when the attackers identify the overlap and move the ball in that direction, the defenders, numbering up from the outside, slide across to cover, and the advantage disappears. It is actually a little more complicated than just moving the ball out to the widest player. Sure, every player who receives the ball should run straight to fix a defender, but he needs to keep watching the defence to assess whether the 'numbers' option is still on.

As long as the attacking players know which defender *should* be marking them, they will have a better idea of when the defence is stretched, and if the overlap still exists. To know

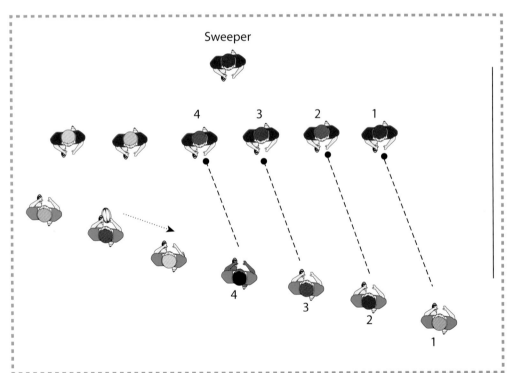

FIGURE 1.1
Attackers develop an awareness of where they stand in the attacking line, in relation to the sideline, and then identify their marker in the defence.

who is marking you, you must first know where *you* stand in the attacking alignment – that is in terms of numbers, and specifically of how many players you are 'in' from the sideline. For example, if you are the third attacker 'in' from the sideline, then the third defender 'in' from the sideline *should* be marking you. This sounds basic, but it still demands that players count to gain the necessary level of awareness.

If the second defender 'in' runs to tackle you, as the third 'in' attacker, you know that there will be an overlap outside. Similarly, if the third defender 'in' runs past you, to defend the player outside you, you know he has *over-tracked*. 'Tracking' is the term used for a defender's *inside* approach to a tackle; *over*-tracking is when the defender runs beyond the player he is marking, creating an opportunity for the ball carrier on his inside, or for other attackers on the other side of the field. This will be examined in detail in Lesson 5 on Defence. From an attacking perspective, being able to exploit a defender who has over-tracked is a valuable skill.

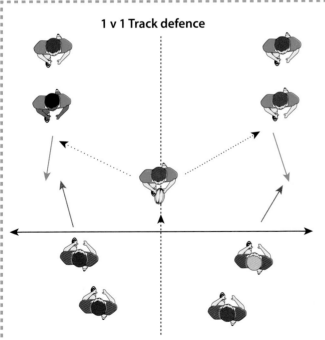

1 v 1 Track defence

- A halfback passes both left and right to start the drill.
- The defender nominates, tracks and tackles the first receiver.
- The attacker runs forward and checks to see if his opponent has over-tracked.
- The drill can also be practice for the halfback running off the ruck.

FIGURE 1.2

Depending on the complexity of the situation, or numbers involved, an overlap in rugby can be over-valued. There is obviously an overlap in a 7 v 6 situation, but it is certainly not an easy equation to solve on the field. The key to exploiting an overlap is to *simplify* this 7 v 6 equation. 6 v 5 is still too difficult; 5 v 4 is likely to require a complex movement pattern; 4 v 3 is workable but still beyond a moderate skill level; 3 v 2 is achievable and familiar territory; but a 2 v 1 is the *ideal* overlap. In attack, we should be looking for 2 v 1s everywhere in the game. Sometimes they will exist on the edges of the defensive line; sometimes we need to use the attacking movement patterns in Lesson 2 to create 2 v 1s in the middle of the field; and sometimes we can take contact to divide the defensive line, and create simpler

and more achievable equations. Split field rucks present the best opportunity to exploit the numerical advantage, and these can be achieved through employing a simple team structure. This will be presented in detail in Lesson 3.

'Equals!'

The opposite of 'numbers' is 'equals' - when the defence manages to *equate* numbers with the attack. Good defences force this scenario on to the attack often, especially following wide rucks, when the sideline does an effective job of *covering* one side of the ruck, allowing the defence to number up on the attack.

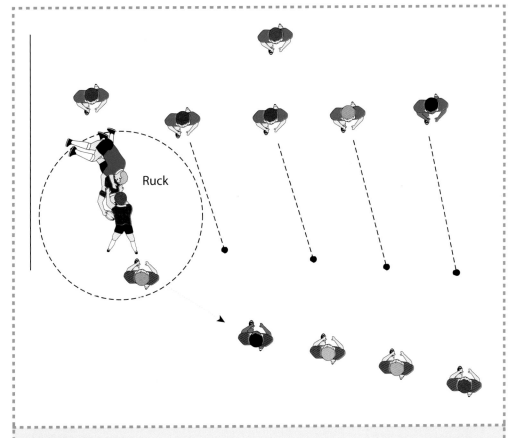

FIGURE 1.3
Wide rucks rarely present the overlap to the attacking team.

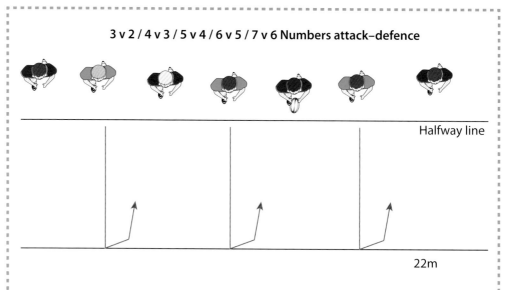

3 v 2 / 4 v 3 / 5 v 4 / 6 v 5 / 7 v 6 Numbers attack–defence

Halfway line

22m

- The same set-up can be used for a 3 v 2, 4 v 3, 5 v 4, 6 v 5, 7 v 6.
- The attackers play the ball when defenders reach the 10m line and turn to defend.
- The drill continues for a set number of phases, or until the attack score. The more players in the drill, the more phases they are allowed to try to score.

FIGURE 1.4

The full value of the attacking movement patterns is seen and experienced when numbers are equal. To simplify decision-making, the attacking players should be constantly assessing the defence, and counting, to determine whether they have more numbers than the defence, or whether numbers are equal. And if they have equal numbers, the attackers should recognise who is marking them and then use the attacking movement patterns in Lesson 2 to beat the defence. If they have more numbers, they call 'Numbers', move the ball and race the defence to space.

An awareness of numbers on the field highlights the complete range of attacking skills for the game – alignment, scanning, communication, decision-making, passing and running with the ball.

LESSON 1: SEVENS IS A NUMBER GAME

Checklist

☐   Numbering up

☐   'Numbers!'

☐   'Equals!'

2 KNOW WHO IS MARKING YOU

One of the top lessons to learn in sevens is to know who is marking you. This may seem like common sense, but it is not coached as often as it should be, at least not with the right emphasis or level of detail. If you know who is marking you, then you know whom to beat.

If you were unsure who was marking you, you would also be unsure about what course of action to take, certainly with any real purpose or precision. It is quite customary for defenders to *nominate* attackers to be sure that they have all threats covered, especially the ball carrier. I would say it is just as important for attackers to nominate defenders to be sure they are aware of all opportunities before them, and especially be aware of which defender is marking the ball carrier.

Importantly, the attacking movement patterns can be called and run spontaneously at any time because they involve only the players either side of the ball carrier. The movements do not require any sophisticated channel of communication to transfer the decision to wider players – just one quick call.

Attacking movement patterns force defenders to move and make decisions in order to create space and attacking opportunities. They are based on the principle that we know how defenders move. Defenders may not like to think that they are so predictable, but the fact is that they are. Think of a one-on-one situation; we know that wherever the ball carrier runs, the defender has to follow. We also know that if the ball carrier runs left, space is created on the right; if the ball carrier runs right, space is created on the left. This may seem overly basic but it is an essential part of any player's education for understanding space in the game.

1 + 1 v 1 Attack–defence

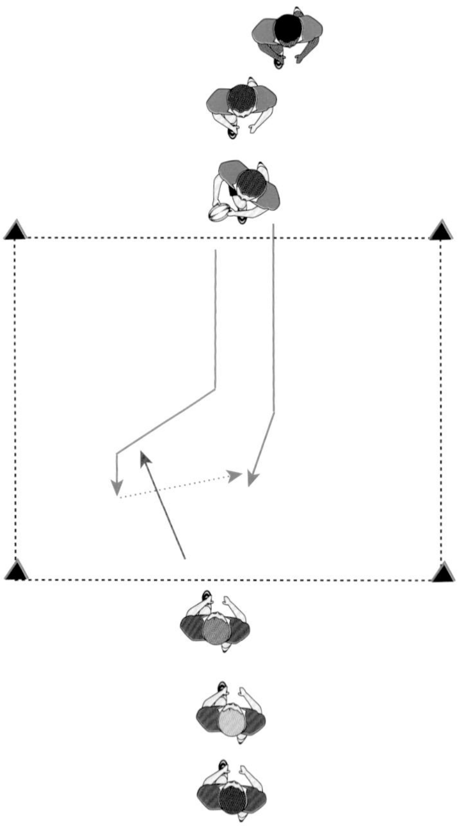

- Attackers and defenders on opposite ends of a grid.
- The ball carrier uses speed and footwork to beat his opponent.
- If tackled, he rides the tackle and aims to offload to his support player.
- The defender aims to track and effect a tackle, preventing the offload if possible.
- The ball carrier can only use the support player after contact, to encourage a 1 v 1 and offload.

FIGURE 2.1

The attacking movement patterns are equally successful whether defenders are organised or stretched; in fact the more organised the defenders are, the easier they are to manipulate, because it is clear who they are marking and we can better anticipate how they will move. Slow ball, quick ball, it doesn't matter – the attacking movement patterns work in every situation.

2 v 2 Attacking movement patterns

'STAY-OUT'

A 'stay-out' is the go-to play in the game. It is the easiest of all the attacking movement patterns for players to understand, and the one that appeals to a generic rugby skill set. As soon as the ball carrier has identified which defender is marking him, he is then ready to run the play. In a nutshell, the ball carrier aims to fix and then beat his opponent on the outside. Look at the line of run of the ball carrier (A1) below:

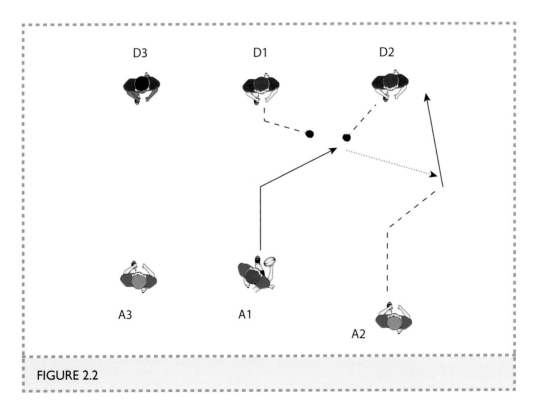

FIGURE 2.2

The ball carrier runs straight at his opponent and then changes direction sharply to beat him on the outside. It is essential that the ball carrier run with the intention to beat his opponent, and not just run across field with no conviction. The outside defender (D2) will have to decide whether to come in to tackle the ball carrier or stay out on the outside attacker (A2). Whichever he chooses, the attack has a chance to break the line. If the defender decides to leave the player he is marking and come in to tackle the ball carrier, the ball carrier executes a simple 2 v 1, where the outside attacker (A2) hits a flat, well-timed pass at pace.

In most cases, the outside defender (D2) will stay out on his man, and so if the ball carrier is quicker than his opponent (D1), he will break through the line. To enhance this, the attacking player outside should mirror the angle of the ball carrier to try and draw his opponent away from the ball, increasing the chances of the ball carrier breaking the line. However, as long as the ball carrier runs with the right intention – to beat his marker – then it does not matter whether or not the defender (D1) is quick enough to cover him. His action of chasing the ball carrier across the field will create space on the *inside* that can be exploited – specifically with a *switch*.

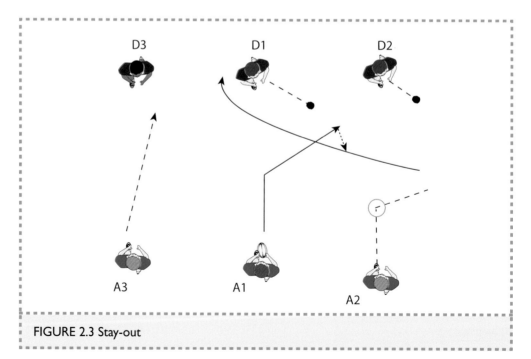

FIGURE 2.3 Stay-out

The outside attacker (A2) should keep reading the situation between the ball carrier and his opponent, to judge if or when he needs to change his angle to run a switch. This is essential to achieve the correct timing of the switch. Switch too early and the defender will hold to cover the player running into his channel; switch too late and the ball carrier will be caught before the switch pass has been completed. If the outside attacker reads the play *correctly*, the switch will be perfect – not too late and definitely not too early! The simple rule is that if the ball carrier is about to get caught, the support player should run the switch. The habit we want to develop is that whenever a player runs into another player's channel, the outside player *looks* for a switch, but may not actually run it, depending on his reading of the situation.

Because we know how defenders move, we should exploit every opportunity to manipulate them. For example, we know that when the defenders see a switch, they will hold their channel to cover the play – that is, the player marking the ball carrier (D1) will hold to cover the player running into his channel (A2). So, as soon as the ball carrier changes direction, A2 should briefly turn his body towards the ball carrier to give the impression that he is going to run a switch, and then he should turn back sharply to stay on the outside. This action is called a 'shake' and should be accompanied by a loud call of 'Switch!' There is a good chance that the defenders will be fooled, and hold in anticipation of the switch. The momentary pause in their movement can be just enough to present the ball carrier (A1) with a great opportunity to break through the line.

If the ball carrier is still covered after the shake, the outside player should then, and only then, run and call for a 'late' switch. The call 'Late' should reflect the priority on the timing of the switch. If players *call* switches, then they just tend to run what they think a 'switch' should look like, and this usually excludes any of the above detail or purpose that is necessary to break the line successfully. Good switches are based on the principles of the ball carrier trying to *beat* his opponent, and the support player reading the play to achieve perfect timing. Players should generally avoid throwing the *dummy* switch in sevens, as this often isolates the ball carrier, and flattens support play.

As in all attacking movement patterns, angle changes should be as dynamic as possible to give defenders little chance to adjust. So with all of this combined, you have a great attacking play, and one that is quick to call and very difficult to defend.

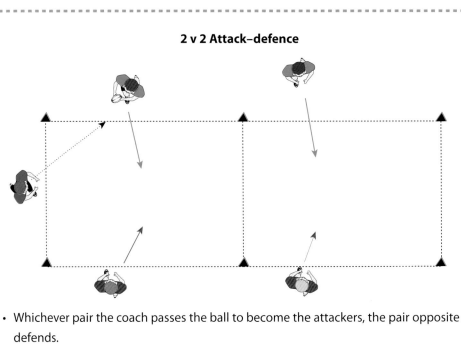

2 v 2 Attack–defence

- Whichever pair the coach passes the ball to become the attackers, the pair opposite defends.
- The attackers try to beat the defence with the attacking movement patterns.
- There is no limit on width.

FIGURE 2.4

'SHORT-BALL'

Sevens is not a complicated game, and there are not many different ways to defend. It is, therefore, not difficult to predict how defenders will move and react in game situations. If defenders do not move as expected, it often means that they have made an error, and given the attack a different opportunity to take advantage of. What makes the attacking movement patterns so deadly is that they are built on manipulating the way we know good defensive teams will operate.

The 'short-ball' is an easy play to understand, and is common in fifteens. The drawback of familiarity is bad habits. Players are likely to need to review their understanding of how to execute a 'short-ball', in order to run it with the appropriate purpose and detail in timing and angles.

Players should strive for perfect 'short-balls' every time the play is called. Players first need to know who is marking them, and *fix* the defenders by running straight at them. The attackers should want the defenders to be clear about whom they are marking, so the space and opportunities around them are clear to see. If I look and run straight at you, it is highly likely that you will look and run straight at me, and the space to attack will be well defined; the same goes for the support player in a 2 v 2 situation. While the 'stay-out' is an angle change by the ball carrier, the 'short-ball' is an angle change by the support runner. In a 'short-ball', the ball carrier runs straight at his marker to fix and hold him on his line of run, and the support player runs at an angle into the space between the two defenders. Sound simple? It is. But it is not simple to do it perfectly every single time, and the 'wrap', which is the crux of the play, needs practice.

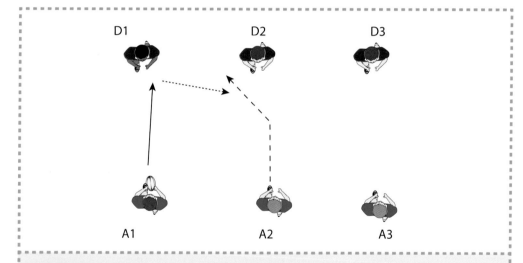

FIGURE 2.5

A1 runs straight to fix his defender; A2 runs an angle into the space between the two defenders.

The support runner (A2) should aim to dissect the defenders exactly, aiming for the very centre of the gap between them. This may seem straightforward but it is not as easy as it sounds if the defenders are sliding across the field. Players will quickly learn that it is more advantageous to attack against a front-on defence, when the gaps are fixed, than a sliding defence, when the gaps are always moving.

As soon as the ball carrier passes to the support runner, he should 'wrap' around the receiver. The sequence is simply: run straight, pass while running straight, and then wrap the receiver. The passer must not start the wrap until he has released the ball. It is common that the passer will take the shortcut of turning towards the support player as he passes, knowing that he has to complete the wrap, but it is vital that he keeps running *straight* to preserve the space between the defenders.

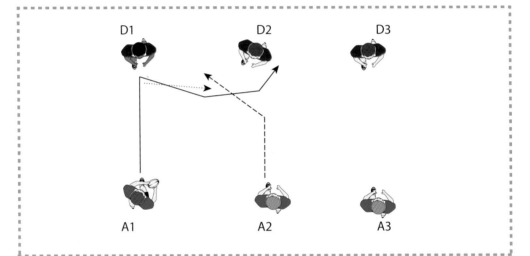

FIGURE 2.6 Short-ball

A1 passes whilst running straight, then wraps around the receiver.

The support player (A2) should catch the ball in two hands and have made a decision whether or not to give the ball back to the player on the wrap (A1). The support player's decision is influenced by the defence – if the defender marking him (D2) has moved in to make the tackle, which is expected, then he gives the pass to A1 on the wrap. If he senses that his angle change and line of run has beaten the defender, he should keep the ball and make the break. The pass back must be an *inside* pass, so that he can keep sight of his target, and be thrown almost immediately into the path of the player on the wrap. Time on the ball is limited on receiving a 'short-ball', as it is a high-speed play, right on the tackle line.

It is this wrapping of the receiver on a 'short-ball', which is the important new habit that needs to be developed (in both sevens *and* fifteens). The wrap effectively gives the attacking team an extra player, turning a 2 v 2 into a 3 v 2, and ensures attackers can always take advantage when the defenders cover the 'short-ball'. The habit of wrapping a 'short-ball' should happen *every* time a pass is made to a player running an 'in' line (also termed *unders* line). Seems simple, but players should be sure to acknowledge and not overlook the principle of knowing who is marking them, so they know who to beat!

'YOU-AND-ME'

The 'you-and-me' is another attacking movement pattern which exploits established defensive systems. Like all of the movement patterns, it demands knowledge of who is marking you, and a clear understanding of how defenders move. The 'you-and-me' is basically an inside ball with a wrap and, like the 'short-ball', it is the wrap that effectively beats the defence.

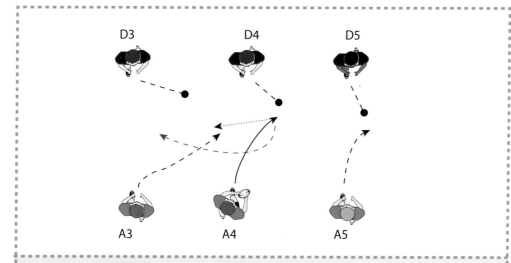

FIGURE 2.7 You-and-me
The red arrow shows the running line of A4 *after* he has made the pass.

The attackers should, first and foremost, aim to run a brilliant inside ball. This demands that the ball carrier aims to beat his opponent on the outside. If he runs with this sense of purpose, he has the best chance of stretching the defence and creating space for the inside support runner. The support player himself should fully commit to his line of run and intend to break the line off the inside pass. If the support player runs with this conviction, it gives the defence little chance to respond to the impending change of direction of the wrap.

Moving 2 v 2 attack–defence

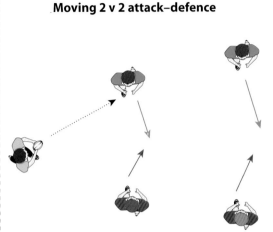

- There are no cones to mark the drill; players are just instructed to stand opposite each other for a 2 v 2, as illustrated.
- The coach runs in random directions, and players have to keep their alignment.
- Whichever pair the coach passes to is the attacking team.
- Once the coach passes the ball, the drill becomes a simple 2 v 2 practice.

FIGURE 2.8

The ball carrier (A4) calls the 'you-and-me' with the player inside him (A3), and then attacks the space outside his opponent (D4). The 'you-and-me' call is a signal for the inside player to run the inside ball, which is effectively the same running angle as the ball carrier. We know how defenders defend an inside ball – that one defender tracks across to tackle the ball carrier, while the inside defender moves to cover the inside runner. This is assuming that the attackers have taken the play close to the tackle line to commit the defenders appropriately. When we know who is marking us and we know how they will move to defend us, the space to attack becomes very clear. The covering defender (D3) has to move across to close the gap for the inside runner, which forces the whole defensive line to slide across to stay connected to him. Immediately after giving the inside pass, A4 quickly runs around the inside runner (A3) and receives the ball back at once, executing what could be termed an *inside-wrap*. This stretches the defence and creates either a line break for the ball carrier or an overlap further out.

The inside ball effectively misleads the defenders about the target area for attack. They see the inside ball happening, and they assume this is the intended play of attack. When the attacker receives the ball back on the inside-wrap, he must quickly scan the defence to identify where the space is. If the defenders have failed to adjust, there will be an opportunity for the ball carrier to break the line immediately; and if the whole defensive line slides across to cover the inside pass, as it should do, space will be created further out, and the ball carrier should quickly move the ball out wide to exploit the overlap.

The 'you-and-me' can work everywhere on the field, but is best run by players around the middle of the field. When the ball is in the middle of the field, the defensive line remains flat, which works well for the inside ball and inside-wrap of the 'you-and-me'. When the ball is out wide, the defensive line tends to hinge on the last defender, which positions defenders in passing channels and disrupts the inside ball. A hinging defence will be discussed in detail in Lesson 5 (*see* pages 78–80).

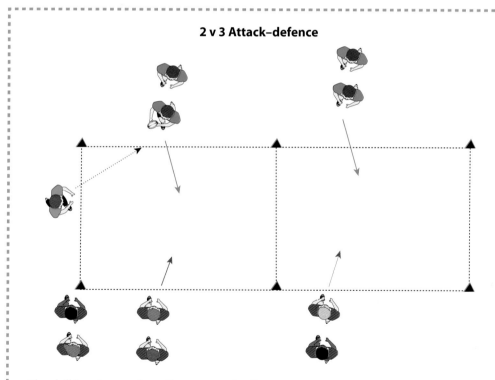

2 v 3 Attack–defence

- The drill is set up and run the same as 2 v 2.
- There are three defenders; the third is just to provide inside cover and is not marking a specific attacker.

FIGURE 2.9

'RUN-ROUND-ME'

We know that wherever an attacking player moves, the defender marking him has to move too, and we can use this simple understanding to manipulate and beat defences. A 'loop' in rugby terms is when an attacking player passes the ball and runs around the receiver. The difference between a loop and a wrap is that a loop is visible to the opposition, while the wrap is aimed to be sudden enough to beat the defence. The way defenders adjust to cover a loop can be anticipated and exploited.

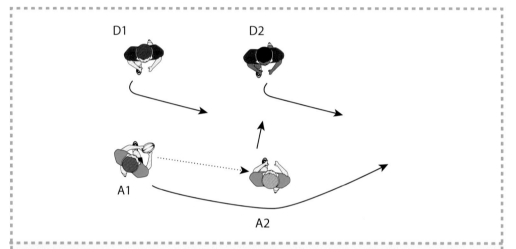

FIGURE 2.10
A1 passes to A2 and loops around him as quickly as possible.

As soon as the defender sees the passer (A1) loop, the defenders will number up from the outside. D1 will slide out to cover the receiver (A2), and the outside defender (D2) will slide out to cover A1. The looping player should aim to move as quickly as possible to force the defenders to also move at pace. Defenders moving sideways at speed are vulnerable to inside steps and passes, and this idea is precisely what is exploited in a 'run-round-me'.

It is important that players distinguish between a loop and a wrap, and acknowledge that, in a 'run-round-me', the attacker is not trying to beat the defence with his movement but running to create opportunities for the player he is looping around. The attacker wants the defenders to see him loop and have time to slide across to cover him on the outside because, in so doing, opportunities will open up on the inside. The ball carrier must keep

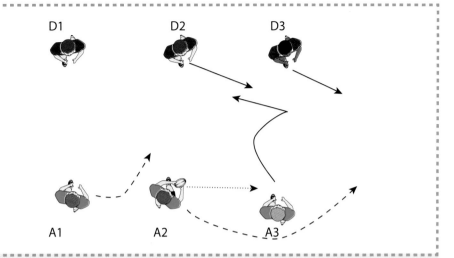

FIGURE 2.11 Run-round-me

A3 has the option to pass outside, step inside the defender, or pass to an inside support runner (A1).

watching how the defenders move because his actions are determined by their *reactions* to the loop. Obviously, if they do not slide to cover the looping player, then there will be a clear overlap on the outside for the attackers to exploit with ease.

As the defenders slide to cover the loop, the player receiving the ball (A3) has a number of options available to him, and must make a decision based on the speed and angle of the defenders' approach. If the defender (D2) is slow to react, the ball carrier may be able to beat him on the outside. Most often, however, the defender will move across quickly to cover the ball carrier, which may prevent an outside break but does present the ball carrier with a simple option to step inside him to break the defensive line. The ball carrier (A3) should importantly *sell* the outside option to the defence, by shaping to pass to the player who has looped outside him. This action is very effective in encouraging the defence to slide quickly, which is exactly what the attack manipulates in a 'run-round-me'.

It is important that the attackers aim to maintain forward momentum as they complete this attacking movement pattern. This makes the timing a little more difficult as the attack will encounter the defence more quickly, but it ensures that the defence does not seize the initiative against a static attack. Players have a tendency to slow down when running this play, which allows defenders to stay balanced and, consequently, become more difficult to beat.

Overall, the 'run-round-me' offers a simple way to unsettle defences and force them to adjust. It is the predictability of this adjustment that provides the attacking opportunities, again centred on knowing who is marking you at any given time.

'QUICK-SWITCH'

Since there is little room for innovation in sevens defence, it is relatively easy to predict how defenders are going to react to a situation. This common knowledge can be used to manipulate and beat defenders. To defend a switch, for example, the defender marking the ball carrier will usually stop chasing the ball, hold his position, and shift his focus to covering the player running into his channel. This defender effectively has to pause momentarily, while he adjusts his focus and angle of run, and this is what we aim to exploit in a 'quick-switch'.

When a switch is executed very late and very close to the tackle line, it is extremely difficult to defend because the defenders are committed to a tackle with no time to adjust to the change of ball carrier. This is the kind of switch that may happen in a 'stay-out' (*see* pages 25–28).

In a 'quick-switch', the ball carrier calls the movement *early*, to allow the defence to *see* the switch happening. The ball carrier runs quite a flat angle to give the outside support player as much time and space as possible to complete the movement pattern. It is important that after making the switch pass, the attacker (A1) works hard to reload into a wide and deep position as quickly as possible to stay alive in the attack.

The outside support player (A2) should run an angle straight towards the defender who has held his channel (D1), to make the defender feel comfortable that he has covered the intended attack. The attacker should take the switch pass at speed to fix the defender. A2 then sharply changes both his angle and pace, and attacks back out towards the original ball carrier. He needs to carefully consider the timing of this angle change; if he alters direction too early, the defender will be able to cover him before he breaks through the line, while if he steps too late he will be tackled. It effectively becomes a race between A2 and

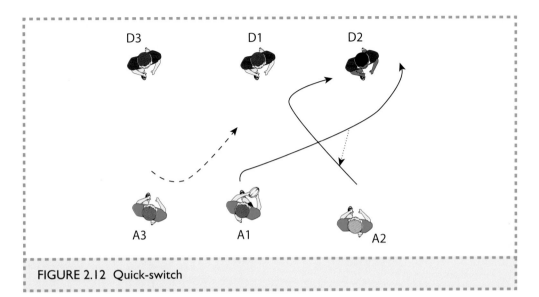

FIGURE 2.12 Quick-switch

D1 to get to the space outside. The initiative is with the ball carrier (A2) since he knows that he is going to change direction, while the defender (D1) has to wait and then react to try to catch up.

As soon as the ball carrier changes direction, the movement becomes a 'stay-out', with the option to run a *second* switch, but this time a 'late' one. The defender who has scrambled to cover the 'quick-switch' is rarely able to adjust his run again to defend the second switch if it is run at pace and with the correct timing.

'PUT-AWAY'

A 'put-away' is effectively a wrap, where the pass is made in contact, and the defender's commitment to the tackle is exploited. The 'put-away' aims to take the defence by surprise. Like many of the attacking movement patterns, the actual movement involved in the 'put-away' already exists in the game, but generally not as a prearranged movement. When these movement patterns are practised repetitively in training, and then run with the appropriate intent and purpose in games, the coordination and timing of support play is so much quicker.

The 'put-away' works on the idea of playing *behind* the defence. Defences work hard to keep organised when the ball is in front of them, but their structure breaks down when the attack manages to get in behind the defensive line. An offload in the tackle to a support player hitting the ball at pace is a simple but extremely effective way to break a defence. And the 'put-away' is effectively just this – an offload in the tackle with support – but where the offload and support is coordinated and not spontaneous. Most offloads happen in a game on impulse, when the ball carrier frees his arms in a tackle and has close support running on to the ball. The 'put-away' is a play that ensures both of these things happen from one simple call.

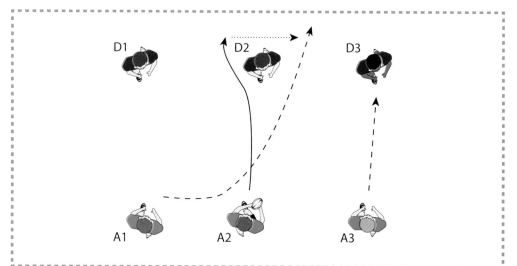

FIGURE 2.13
A2 must show dynamic footwork to evade his marker and keep his arms free for the offload.

The ball carrier must first identify which defender is marking him, and then let the inside player know his intention ('Hey, John, I'm going to put you away'). Remember the simple lesson of when the ball carrier runs right, space is created on the left and vice versa. In a 'put-away', the ball carrier identifies which defender is marking him, steps inside the defender, engaging him in a tackle, and then makes an immediate offload to a support runner hitting space outside.

In a 'put-away', it is not necessary for the ball carrier to beat the defender outright, but just to get to his inside and stretch him enough to make any tackle a passive one, which allows the offload. The success of the offload will be determined by the quality of the run, and so the ball carrier must aim to be as dynamic as possible in the way he moves. He should also maintain leg drive through contact and aim to keep the ball in two hands to make the offload.

The timing between the ball carrier and the inside support player is critical because a 'put-away' is played *through* the tackle, and there is risk of losing the ball in contact. The offload has to be made almost immediately after contact, so if the support player (A1) runs too late, the move will break down. If he runs too early the defence will move to cover both him and the space targeted for attack. The support player *must* wait until the ball carrier steps inside the defender, and only then race to the space outside to take the offload. It is also important that the support player runs a line as close to the tackler as possible, to avoid being covered by other defenders and to make the pass in contact as simple as possible.

The outside support player (A3) plays a role to preserve the space inside. As soon as the 'put-away' is called, he should stay wide and move up flat with the ball carrier. The flatter his position, the more likely it is that his marker (D3) will stay fixed on him. This also puts him nearer to the tackle as a support player in case the move breaks down. He can also call for the ball to draw his opponent's attention and deter him from moving in to cover the offload to A1.

The 'put-away' is a simple play, built on the principle of knowing who is marking you, but it is one that needs practice to correct timing.

'LAZY'

A 'lazy' is an attacking movement pattern that confuses defenders. As with the 'quick-switch', defenders feel no apparent threat, then suddenly they find themselves out of position, locked on to the wrong attackers, and the ball carrier is running through them.

In a 'lazy', the ball carrier runs exactly lateral, not forward, in front of the support player outside him. He then turns back to play an inside ball to the same support player who he ran in front of (A2). What makes this play work is that, in most cases, the defender (D2) will hold on A2, when he *should* actually slide out to cover the ball carrier (A1). It is important that the support player initially holds his position to allow the ball carrier to run across the front of him. Both players then look to change the pace of the attack, running for and *selling* the inside ball to the defence. Specifically, the ball carrier shapes to pass back inside to

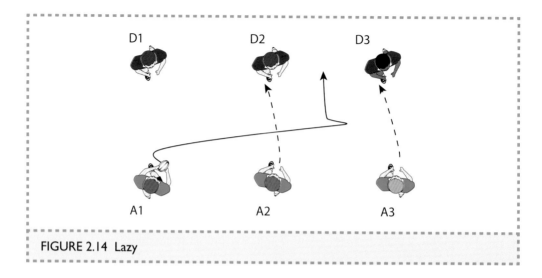

FIGURE 2.14 Lazy

the support player, who calls for and runs hard at the inside line. The outside attacker (A3) contributes to the play by holding a wide position, which keeps his defender away from the targeted area of attack.

The gap *should* open up for the ball carrier, but if it doesn't, regardless of how the defenders react, there will always be an opportunity to make a break somewhere. If D3 comes in, the ball carrier (A1) can make a simple outside pass. If the defence slide correctly, with D2 covering A1, he can throw the inside pass to A2. As with the 'you-and-me', and all inside passes in sevens, players should wrap the pass – effectively turning a 'lazy' into a 'you-and-me'.

The successful combination or stacking of attacking movement patterns proves an advanced level of understanding in attacking play. A simple 2 v 2 grid is the most staple drill for the game, and will have the biggest effect on the success of your team in attack and defence.

LESSON 2: KNOW WHO IS MARKING YOU

Checklist

- ☐ 'Stay-out'
- ☐ 'Short-ball'
- ☐ 'You-and-me'
- ☐ 'Run-round-me'
- ☐ 'Quick-switch'
- ☐ 'Put-away'
- ☐ 'Lazy'

3

PLAY WITH STRUCTURE

Sevens can be extremely physically demanding, so teams should aim to play the game as efficiently as possible. Compared to fifteens, the ball is in play for longer periods of time, with fewer stoppages and fewer opportunities to recover. The answer to these challenges is to adopt a structured approach to the game.

Link structure

The *link structure* is the basic pattern for every sevens team, and one that should be introduced right at the beginning of

Structure does not stifle flair; it gives players a framework on the field that allows them to express their skills with confidence, knowing that there is a model to revert to when play becomes disorganised. Establishing a framework in which players have clearly defined roles and responsibilities also makes our job as coaches easier. It presents a clear picture of how play should look, making our task of problem solving and error correction much simpler.

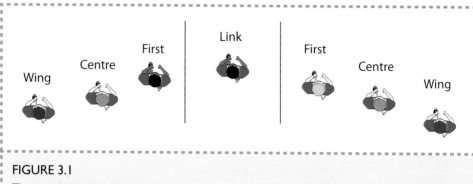

FIGURE 3.1

The coach should use these titles to refer to a player in a specific position in general play – e.g. 'John, when find yourself at "first", you need to look up and see who is marking you.'

any training programme. The structure instantly establishes width and efficiency in support play, and importantly promotes *support in threes*, a principle that will be presented in detail in Lesson 4. In the link structure, two attacking units of three players operate either side of a *link* player, producing a 3-1-3 formation.

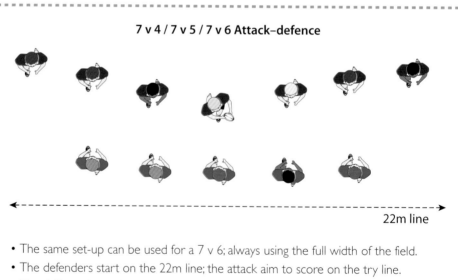

7 v 4 / 7 v 5 / 7 v 6 Attack–defence

22m line

- The same set-up can be used for a 7 v 6; always using the full width of the field.
- The defenders start on the 22m line; the attack aim to score on the try line.
- The drill continues for a set period of time, after which the players change roles.

FIGURE 3.2

The primary role of the link player is to move the ball between the two attacking units, facilitating a seesawing style of attack – while one unit attacks on one side of the field, the other unit reloads for their turn to attack on the other side of the field. Think of the field as divided into three channels. The link player maintains a position in the central channel of the field, wide and deep enough to act as a pivot between the two units who operate in the wider channels either side.

It is not uncommon for players to get pulled out of position in sevens, as play continues and fatigue sets in, so every player in the team should develop a good understanding of the link structure, and gain experience in all positions across the team, especially at link. The general rule is that whenever the link player is drawn into contact, another player should fill the role so that the team structure continues. This process of fluidly replacing the link player, and continuously regenerating the structure after it has broken down, is the key to this structured approach.

Double-depth

As each unit attacks and recycles the ball in their channel, the link takes up the position as first receiver off the ruck, setting the depth and alignment for the attacking unit of three players outside him. Importantly, the player at first position in the unit outside the link should set his depth as if the link player is another ruck (and not a first receiver), to establish *double-depth* from the actual ruck. If the player at 'first' is flat on the link player, the attacking unit will have insufficient depth – that is, time and space – to run plays.

An effective activity to practise setting up the link structure from set pieces is to play ten consecutive scrums, allowing play to flow for strictly one minute at a time; then ten consecutive lineouts, playing for strictly one minute at a time, or until the attack scores. This timed approach fosters the repetition needed to acquire the necessary skills and understanding from set pieces. The same can be applied to kick offs, penalties and free kicks.

Attacking players on the *outside* should communicate to inside players about maintaining depth in their alignment. When outside players take responsibility for the alignment and depth of players inside them, they maximise their own chances of getting the ball.

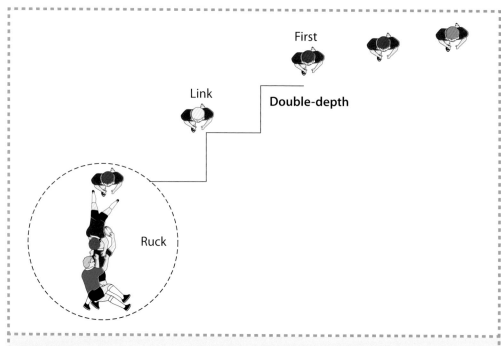

FIGURE 3.3

The player at first in the attacking unit establishes double-depth off the ruck, by setting his depth as if the link player himself is another ruck.

The link structure is one that can be established quickly and easily from restarts in the game. From a scrum or a lineout, for example, the three forwards win the set piece, and then reload as an attacking unit, on their side of the field. The halfback runs into the central link position, and immediately has a unit of forwards on one side of him and a unit of backs on the other. In the link structure, players notably do not have to run all over the field in support; they just support the players in their attacking unit on *their* side of the field. This gives the team the efficiency it needs to handle the rigours of the game.

It is important to note that the link structure is dependent on the ability of the attacking units to win and clear their own ball in tackle situations – supporting in threes. If they cannot win the ball in contact as a three-player unit, the link has to abandon his central position to assist in clearing the ball, resulting in a negative loss of width in the attacking team.

Whilst the structure and seesawing nature of the attack may seem predictable, it works, and has helped some of the best teams in the world win tournaments.

Optimal plays by combination

The link structure contains only three positional combinations, and it is worth noting that some attacking movement patterns are more suited to certain combinations. For structure, most attacking movement patterns should be played between first and centre and between centre and wing. This allows the link to stay focused on his primary role of shifting the ball between the two units, but he should be encouraged to attack whenever the opportunity presents itself.

It is certainly useful for players to be given the following guide on the most effective attacking movement patterns for their combination:

LINK AND FIRST:
- 'You-and-me'
- 'Short-ball'
- 'Run-round-me'

FIRST AND CENTRE:
- 'You-and-me'
- 'Short-ball'
- 'Put-away'
- 'Lazy'
- 'Run-round-me'

CENTRE AND WING:
- 'Stay-out'
- 'Run-round-me'
- 'Quick-switch'
- 'Put-away'

Secondary support plays: short and doubles

With ready-made support units, the link structure is a great framework for the attacking movement patterns. It also sets a convenient structure to plan *secondary support plays,* effective for when the defence scramble to cover the immediate threat of the attacking movement patterns. For simplicity, these secondary support plays should be reserved for the wider centre-wing attacks, but there is no reason why they cannot work everywhere on the field.

The secondary support plays apply to the player at first position on a centre-wing attack. Certain attacking movement patterns – namely 'stay-out', 'run-round-me', 'you-and-me' – allow this player to run a secondary support play, which serves as an additional strike at

3 v 3 Attack–defence

- Players in threes at opposite ends of a wide grid.
- The drill is best played from the middle of the field to a sideline.
- The attackers try to beat the defence with the attacking movement patterns and secondary support plays.
- The defence number up and use inside cover to prevent a try.

FIGURE 3.4

Structure can be used effectively to manipulate defenders and create space for line breaks.

the defence. After passing to the centre, the player at 'first' stays connected to but does not chase the attack. He watches the defence and reads the play as the centre and wing perform their chosen attacking movement pattern. If either player takes contact, he moves in quickly to secure the ball or play halfback – to keep to the idea of supporting in threes. But when the opportunity arises, when the play comes back towards him, he can run *short* or *doubles* to continue the attacking movement.

A short is simply a 'short-ball', where the player at 'first' runs for a short-ball and gives the wrap pass if necessary. Doubles is where first wraps *around* the ball carrier to the outside. The success of these plays will be determined by the quality of the initial attacking movement pattern.

The decision to run a short or doubles is determined by the state of the defence after the attacking movement pattern. The player at first, or any player who runs for a secondary

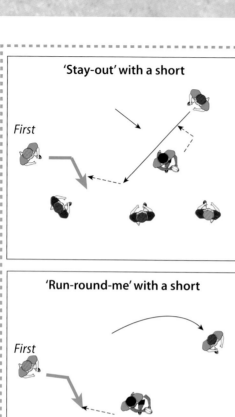

'Stay-out' with a short

First

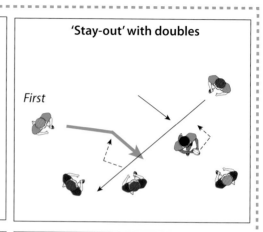

'Stay-out' with doubles

First

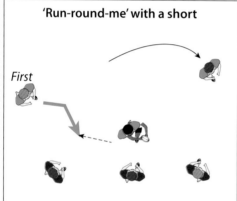

'Run-round-me' with a short

First

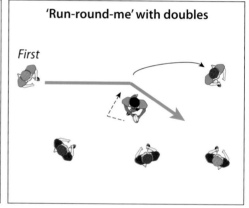

'Run-round-me' with doubles

First

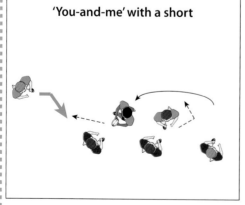

'You-and-me' with a short

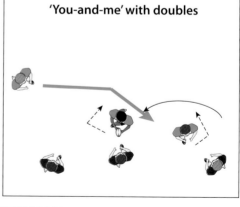

'You-and-me' with doubles

FIGURE 3.5

support play, identifies where space has been created and, reading the current direction of the defenders, looks for the best opportunity to break the line. A general rule seems to be that whenever the attacking movement pattern has stretched but not beaten the defence, a short is the best option to keep the attack moving forward; but when the defence has adjusted well to the initial play – usually as a result of poor timing on the attacking movement pattern – doubles is the play to provide an additional punch to beat the defence out wide.

All players running a short or doubles should aim to provide an injection of pace into the attack, and it is this change of pace, coupled with good decision-making and smart running lines, that makes the secondary support plays so effective. Our goal, through repetition and good coaching, is to advance players to a level of understanding where the secondary support plays are run instinctively.

Situational play

The link structure is most straightforward when the centre or wing takes the ball into contact, as this does not draw the link player into the attack, allowing him to hold his position in the middle of the field. However, when the player at first position attacks, the link player is drawn into the attacking movement as an inside support player, and has to surrender his central position. The same happens when the link himself is caught in contact. In these situations, the 3–1–3 formation breaks down, but does present other attacking opportunities and the structure can always be restored quickly within one phase of play.

There are only a limited number of possible scenarios on the sevens field when the ball is taken into contact. This is assuming that attacking units are always made up of three players – the ball carrier, a contact support player and a halfback.[1] It is a matter of simple mathematics – three players involved in the tackle area leaves four players out in the field. This may sound like common sense, but it is a key revelation on the game and one that is guaranteed to simplify your coaching and accelerate your players' learning.

---

[1] The halfback refers to any player who clears the ball from a ruck.

SCENARIO 1: ATTACK ON LINK

When the link player takes the ball into contact, the nearest players have to support him. This will generally be the player at first position in both attacking units, leaving two 2-player attacking units either side of the ruck. A link attack, therefore, creates a '2–2' split field.

There will be a clear 2 v 2 opportunity on one side of the field, determined by which side the defender behind the ruck chooses to stand on. The option is to play the ball to the 2-player unit who has this clear 2 v 2 opportunity, and revert to the attacking movement patterns for an attacking play.

The link structure can be quickly restored, crucially after only one phase. Whoever clears the ball as halfback at the centrefield ruck, *joins* the players that he passes to – recreating a 3-player attacking unit. The two players from the ruck reload into a 3–1–3 formation, with one of the players assuming the link role.

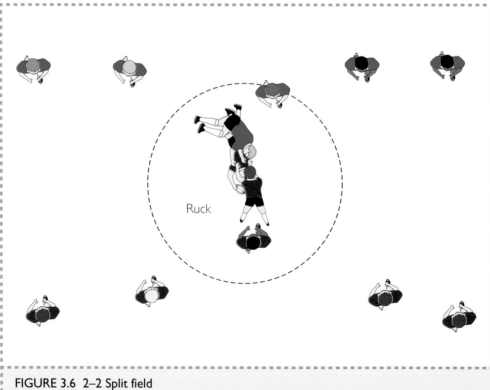

Ruck

FIGURE 3.6 2–2 Split field

SCENARIO 2: ATTACK ON FIRST

When the player at first position takes the ball into contact, the link and centre are the players usually expected to support the attack. This leaves a complete 3-player attacking unit on one side of the field, and just one player, usually the wing, on the other side of the field. An attack on first creates a valuable 3-1 split field.

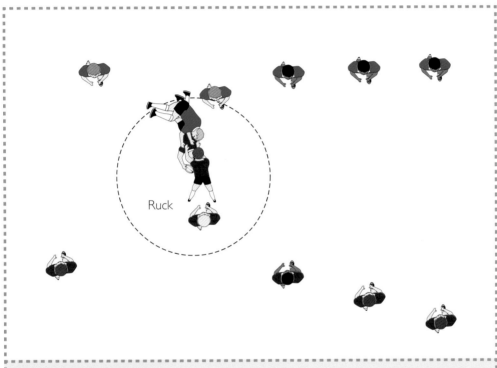

Ruck

FIGURE 3.7 3–1 Split field

The halfback can either pass to the 3-player attacking unit on one side of the ruck, or run the ball towards the wing on the other side. On the halfback's approach to the ruck, both he and the wing should be looking to see if there is an opportunity to join forces for an easy 2 v 1 play. Basically, if the opposition has two players on the same side of the ruck as the wing, the best option is to pass back to the 3-player attacking unit. If they only have one defender marking the wing, the halfback should run to draw the defender and put the wing into space. Specifically, his cue is the defender behind the ruck – the halfback should play the ball to the opposite side that he is standing on.

The play to the wing is similar to a simple 'stay-out', except where the halfback's aim is to draw the outside defender rather than beating a specific opponent of his own. If the option is to play the attacking unit of 3-players, the attackers should use and combine the attacking movement patterns and secondary support plays to beat the defence.

The link structure can again be restored after only one phase. If the halfback passes to the 3-player attacking unit, the 3-1-3 is established almost immediately. If he chooses to attack with the wing, one player from the ruck must quickly join them to follow the principle of supporting in threes. The other player from the ruck reloads as link in the middle of the field, and the 3-1-3 formation is restored.

SCENARIO 3: ATTACK ON WING

When the wing takes the ball into contact, the other players in his attacking unit move to support him. The link player can hold his wide position in the middle of the field, between the two attacking units of three players. An attack on the wing sets up the link structure more effectively than any other attack, as it does not draw the link player into the attacking movement. A wing attack creates a 4-0 field – four players on one side of the ruck, no players on the other side.

In most instances, the halfback at the ruck should pass to the link, to move the ball to the other attacking unit. He has the option to dart down the short side on his own, but must be certain that he is in the clear as he is sure to be isolated. While an attack on wing facilitates the link structure, a wide ruck is the most difficult scenario to attack from, simply because the defence only has one side of the ruck to defend, and can advance with speed and confidence to shut the attack down.

The attacking unit outside the link should aim for *double-depth* off the ruck (*see* pages XX–XX). If the defence advances quickly, the attack may not have time to move the ball wide enough for a centre–wing attack. They may therefore need to call a play between first and centre, or even link and first, referring to the *optimal plays by combination* above. A rare miss pass from link to centre should also not be ruled out, as it can stretch the defence in this situation, but there is no other scenario where a miss pass is acceptable in the game.

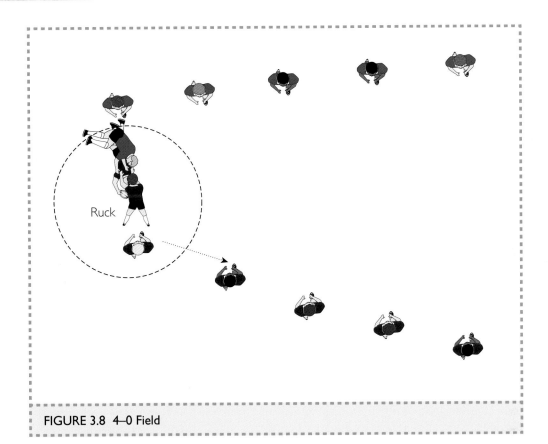

FIGURE 3.8 4–0 Field

SCENARIO 4: ATTACK ON CENTRE

An attack on the centre can result in Scenario 3 or Scenario 4, mainly depending on the width of the attack. If the attack is wide, it makes sense for the wing to commit to supporting the attack, allowing the link to hold his central position (Scenario 3, see figure 3.8).

If it is a tighter attack near the middle of the field, and the wing has held a wide position, it makes sense for the link player to move in to play halfback at the ruck (Scenario 2, see figure 3.7).

An open channel of communication should exist between link and wing for when the centre attacks. If the link is closer to the tackle area, he should tell the wing to stay out, to create a valuable 3-1 split field, which forces the defence to spread and cover the full width of the field.

Advanced link model

When players have grasped the simplicity of the 3-1-3 formation and the security of the link structure, they can then be presented with the more advanced model below.

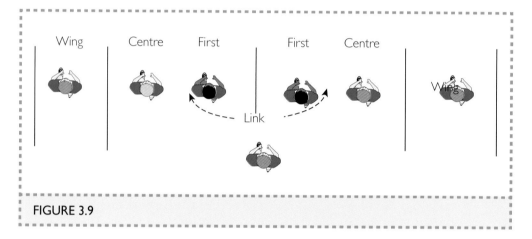

FIGURE 3.9

This illustration presents a more advanced model of the link structure, considering the analysis of the situational play above. It shows how the team actually plays in four channels, not three. In the more advanced structure, the wing should split from his attacking unit and stay wide whenever possible. This creates the valuable 3-1 split field more often, and forces a wider spread in the defence.

The advanced link model identifies the two firsts and centres as the key playmakers and attacking thrusts of the team. They can choose to keep the attacking movement pattern between themselves and exclude the wing from the play, which advantageously sets up the 3-1 split field for the halfback; or the centre can choose to *engage* the wing in an attacking movement pattern, which keeps the attacking unit intact and facilitates the familiar 3-1-3 formation.

In the advanced link model, the halfback plays in a more conventional role of visiting rucks to run off or clear the ball. Importantly, the advanced link model, with its split field focus, positions the halfback to *initiate* and not always *facilitate* the attack. Vital for his own motivation as well as to keep the defence guessing!

LESSON 3: PLAY WITH STRUCTURE

Checklist

☐ Link structure

☐ Double-depth

☐ Optimal plays by combination

☐ Secondary support plays

☐ Short

☐ Doubles

☐ Situational play

☐ Split fields / 4-0 field

☐ Advanced link model

4 SUPPORT IN THREES

Possession in sevens is key to success. The team that can keep and control possession will generally win the game. When considering continuity in sevens, the general rule is that players should support in threes, where three includes the ball carrier. When the ball carrier is tackled to ground, a second player is needed to secure possession, and a third to clear the ball. Every player who is involved in an attacking movement pattern, namely the players either side of the ball carrier, should understand that they have an important role to play when contact is made, and move efficiently to ensure that possession is retained, secured and cleared from pressure.

Teams should be rigorously drilled into preparing to commit three players to every tackle situation. Where there is a threat of a turnover, more players may be needed to win the ball, but on the understanding that if a fourth player has to move in to help secure possession, the attacking team would lose width and options, and the initiative would shift to the defending team. In some instances, there may be no contest at the breakdown at all, so the first arriving player can clear the ball allowing the third player to hold width, but it is just good practice to prepare players to support in threes.

If we have three players on and around the ball at any given time, we are covered if the ball carrier is tackled to ground, but priority should always be given to keeping the ball alive and off the floor. A ruck[2] presents the defence with a great opportunity to contest possession, as well as giving them time to consolidate and reset their defensive line. An offload in the tackle is a much quicker form of managing contact, and gives the defence no time to reset. Attacking players should look to combine with their support wherever possible to make an offload and keep the ball moving.

It is important to acknowledge that success *in* contact is most influenced by what players do *before* contact is made. Players should trust the attacking movement patterns to create and exploit space, but in general accept that the quality of their footwork or running line *before* contact will always determine the quality of any offload *in* contact, and influence the overall efficiency of the ruck if tackled to ground.

The ball carrier should always aim to beat his opponent into space, and to make a clean break. When trying to beat a player in a one-on-one situation or in an attacking movement pattern, a two-step is more dynamic than a simple side-step.[3] A two-step is simply the action of combining two side-steps, one immediately following the other. The ball carrier's first step fakes the direction of attack and aims to shift the defender's balance to one side, and the second step drives him away to the other side. So, to get around the defender on the left, he first steps off his left foot, then off his right; to get around the defender on the right, he steps first off his right, then off his left. Like most evasive skills, the two-step is most effective when performed at pace.

Offload

Offload in or after a tackle is a priority in sevens. This keeps the ball moving, making it difficult for the defence to reset their defensive line, and avoids a contest for possession.

When the ball carrier cannot avoid contact, it is important that he is tackled on his own terms, and he should aim at least to get in behind his tackler with dynamic footwork and fend. If the ball carrier runs straight into a defender, the defender has time and position to

---

[2]A ruck is formed with one player from either team in contact over the ball.
[3]A side-step is the action of stepping dynamically off one foot to change direction.

set up for an aggressive front-on tackle. Front-on tackles limit the chances for an offload; side tackles are more passive and often low enough for the ball carrier to free his arms to make an offload. The momentum and forces involved in a passive tackle favour the ball carrier, keeping the defence on the back foot and allowing the ball carrier to *ride the tackle* to make the offload.

Players should not see a tackle as a failure, but rather be positive about controlling the contact. For example, if a ball carrier is hit from the right, he should ride the tackle and roll with his left shoulder to ground; if hit from the left, he rolls with his right shoulder to ground. This takes advantage of the momentum of the tackler to turn the body towards support for an offload. Developing this understanding will help players approach contact with confidence, and provide a technical focus to distract from any fear of impact. Importantly, one-on-one drills should be practised with support, not only to develop an appreciation of space for support players, but also for the ball carrier to practise the skill of riding the tackle and offloading out of contact; figure 2.1 (page 24) illustrates this well. The 'put-away' (*see* pages 37–39) is also great practice for the skills of the offload and support play.

Support players must work hard off the ball to give the ball carrier options to pass or offload out of the tackle. They should be constantly *reading* the play,

Emile Ntamack, former French national player and coach, gave a world-class presentation at an international coaching conference about anticipation in support play. He described an activity that involved players commentating on play as it unfolds in front of them. Specifically, when the ball carrier feels confident to make a break, he calls, 'Duel!' signalling support players to run at space for an offload. When he sees no opportunity to beat the defence, he calls, 'Contact!' to prepare support players for his approach to contact. This is a brilliant exercise for sevens as there is generally more space and time than in fifteens to assess the defence and make a call. The purpose of the activity is to encourage support players to read the play and increase the speed and accuracy of their decisions in support. Rather than employing this as a calling system in the game, it is a great activity to use in training, to teach support players around the ball carrier that they should stay connected to and synchronised with the attack, supporting in threes to secure the ball.

which means assessing situations as they happen on the field, and making decisions based on the movements of the ball carrier and the state of the defence. Support players should anticipate what is going to happen and back their decision.

Work on ground

There are obviously times when the ball carrier is unable to offload due to the nature of the tackle or because there are no support players running into space either side of him. And it is the very nature of the tackle that influences his actions and decisions. The principle in contact is to 'fight on feet; fight on ground' – fight meaning to work and compete and not be passive in contact. Specifically, the ball carrier should fight forwards on his feet, and then fight backwards on the ground. The ball carrier is chiefly responsible for retaining possession, and accepting this should trigger the work and effort required on impact and on contact with the ground.

When the ball carrier is tackled very quickly to the ground, the laws require him to play the ball immediately. If he has followed the principle of trying to beat his marker, the resulting side-on tackle should enable him to present the ball with more control to his support players. His options are to pop the ball up to a support player or, if support is delayed, roll or throw the ball backwards, which is not ideal but preferable to losing possession. If support is near, which should be the case when supporting in threes, the ball carrier should work hard to achieve as long a place of the ball as possible. Importantly, the tackled player should keep active on the ground – 'fight on ground' – aiming to make the ball accessible to the halfback. He should not become passive on contact with the ground nor stop working to push the ball back until it has been cleared from the ruck. And then he needs to get up and reload with no delay.

There are obvious benefits to leg drive in contact as this promotes the principle of go forward, but in sevens, staying on your feet in contact can slow movement of the ball and attract defenders who can make the ball unplayable. If the ball carrier is held up, or the resulting maul[4] collapses, a scrum is awarded to the defending team, resulting in a negative loss of possession. Either way, there is little advantage in getting caught on your feet in contact for very long.

---

[4]A maul is formed when one player from each team is in contact with the ball carrier whilst he is still on his feet.

When the ball carrier cannot evade a front-on tackle or is held on his feet, he has a couple of options available to him. Conventionally placing the ball back at arms length will give him no advantage in the tackle contest. At junior level, players should roll quickly and immediately on contact with the ground, to sever any opponent's grip on the ball. At senior level, a front-on tackle would be the only time a player should consider dropping to the ground into a squeeze-ball[5] position. The important thing to keep within the laws of the game is to play the ball immediately. Referees will penalise a tackled player who does not roll away or delays playing the ball on the ground.

It is worth noting that there are also times when taking contact is the best option, especially when there is a need to regain structure and depth in the attack. This could be when patterns have broken down, or the defence is right up in the faces of the attackers, blocking passing lanes. In these situations, the ball carrier should seek contact to create an offside line, which importantly forces the opposition to retreat. The attackers must then aim to recycle the ball as quickly as possible before the defenders have time to reorganise and adjust to the attacking alignment.

In a squeeze-ball, the ball carrier achieves a stable position on his forearms and knees facing the opposition, and pushes the ball back through his legs. This serves as an effective way to momentarily protect the ball from the opposition, especially when the tackler is still on his feet threatening a turnover. For safety, players should be coached to keep the forehead off the ground and chin off chest at all times when performing a squeeze-ball. The technique should be considered a contingency plan, performed only when the ball carrier is tackled front-on and at the level of the ball, or held on his feet by one or more defenders. Used at the right times, and executed safely, the squeeze-ball can be a highly effective way to eliminate a tackle contest and guarantee possession at ruck time.

[5]Please note that the squeeze-ball is illegal at all levels of the game from Under 19s and below, but is allowed at senior level, only when the ball is made available immediately.

First support play

When the ball carrier is tackled to ground, the priority for support is simply to reach the tackled player before a defender. Continuity is more about the speed of support than anything else. Players around the ball carrier should read play, anticipate when contact is unavoidable, and move instantaneously to secure possession when contact is made. There is a notable difference, in terms of speed and success in continuity, between support players

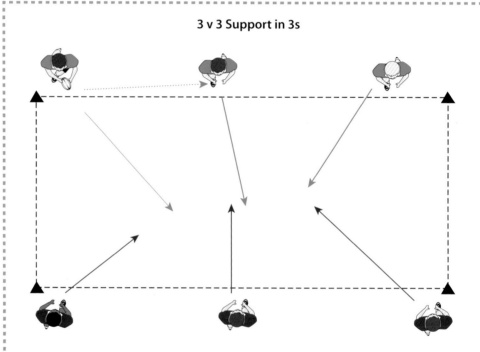

3 v 3 Support in 3s

- 3 v 3; players face each other across a grid.
- Both attackers and defenders must start in a position covering the full width of the grid.
- The width and depth of the grid can be adjusted to target different objectives.
- The attackers pass the ball between them, until one decides to attack.
- The ball carrier aims to evade the tacklers and get in behind the defence to facilitate ruck efficiency.
- Both teams aim to win the tackle contest.

FIGURE 4.1

who anticipate and those who watch and *then* react. Players should participate and not spectate, and realise that if they lose the race to the tackled player, they are most likely to also lose the ball.

Due to the small numbers involved, the tackle area in sevens is relatively straightforward. Whilst speed to the breakdown is the key factor, technical accuracy is essential, not only because of the one-on-one nature of the game, but also because the tackle area is much cleaner than in fifteens, and therefore much easier to referee. Any infringements are clearly visible and quickly penalised. Remember, sevens is rugby magnified – for players, coaches, spectators *and* referees!

There is admittedly a fine line in the interpretation of what is permissible at the breakdown within the laws of the game, and what a referee will penalise in competition, especially when referring to the first support player.[6] The laws of the game stipulate arriving players must be on their feet at the tackle, and this sometimes presents a real challenge to the attacking team. It is fine when there is no contest for the ball. In this case, the first support player either plays the ball immediately or stands over the ball, ready to drive away any defenders who approach. Generally, defenders will not contest possession if an attacker has already won the space over the ball – speed to the ball is key.

It is a very different situation if the attack is beaten to the ball by the tackler himself or another defender. In this situation, the aim of the first support player is simply to hit contact as fast and as low as possible – specifically, to *skim* the tackled player, and *win* the space beyond the ball – *skim and win*. The expectation is that he achieves this and stays on his feet in the contact. The challenge is to achieve a low enough body position to remove the threat of the defender whilst staying within the laws of the game. The level of difficulty depends on the body height of the defender, using the height of the defender's shoulders as a measure. For example, a defender standing upright is obviously easier to move than a defender reaching down with hands on the ball. The general rule is that the shoulders of the first support player need to be *lower* than the defender's shoulders. So a defender who has managed to get his shoulders right down over the ball on the ground can be very difficult to move, which is why speed to the ball in the first place is always the priority.

[6] The first support player is the first attacking player to arrive at the tackle.

LAUNCH

An effective technique specifically for the first support player is the launch. This involves momentarily achieving a 'press-up'[7] position over the ball – where the head and shoulders are beyond the tackled player, and legs and feet straddle the ball. The first support player hits contact with head and shoulders no lower than hips as the law states, targets the press-up position directly over the ball, and then chases his feet through the contact to get back to his feet if necessary. The important thing is that the first support player 'endeavours to stay on his feet',[8] accepting that, in most cases, the impact with the defender will actually prevent him from reaching the ground beyond the tackled player anyway.

However, the reality is that if the first support player is apprehensive about going off his feet, and passive about capturing the ground beyond the tackled player, his technique is likely to be ineffective at moving a defender who is aggressively contesting possession. The first support player must be fully committed to winning the space beyond the tackled player, and the press-up position should be considered just a midpoint in the whole movement not the final destination, but can prove to be the vital ingredient in securing possession.

The launch is certainly open to interpretation, but it will secure more balls than concede penalties. If players misunderstand the technique and dive off their feet when there is no contest on the ball, they deserve to be penalised. The general rule is that if a defender has hands on the ball, the first support player should execute the launch; if not, a conventional cleanout is sufficient. The players must aim for technical accuracy throughout the movement, and specifically focus on lowering hips into and during contact.

It cannot be considered possible, in every situation, for a player to stay on his feet after hitting contact with the necessary speed and body height to secure the ball. The important thing is that he arrives on his feet and endeavours to stay on his feet in the ruck. The launch promotes a safe and stable position throughout the movement – of *shoulders above hips, back flat* and *chin off chest*. It is not a technique designed to achieve an unfair advantage, but one to help the attacking team be more effective in the rigorous tackle contest that is prevalent in the game today.

[7]A press-up, also termed 'push-up', is a position in which only the hands and feet are in contact with the ground, specifically shoulder width apart, with back flat, and head in a neutral position.
[8]Taken from IRB Laws of the Game

We should give players the opportunity in training to manage a range of contact situations, and be careful to condition the intensity of the activities for injury prevention. Full contact drills should run for a very limited time, and over short distances to minimise impact. Once players learn the technique, and prove they can apply it correctly and safely to situations they encounter in the game, and that they understand the principle of supporting in threes, MOVE ON!

LESSON 4: SUPPORT IN THREES

Checklist

☐   Two-step

☐   Riding the tackle

☐   Offload

☐   Fight on feet; fight on ground

☐   Squeeze-ball

☐   Anticipation in support

☐   First support play

☐   Skim and win

☐   Launch

5 DEFEND AS A TEAM

Defence is all about discipline, not in terms of giving away penalties, but in players showing the self-restraint and collective control to play to a strict pattern.

Defence can broadly be broken down into three stages – pre-tackle, the tackle itself, and post-tackle. Pre-tackle is about tracking, keeping the defensive line intact and exerting pressure to force the opposition into contact or making an error; tackle is obviously about choice and execution of the tackle; and post-tackle is first about contesting possession in contact, and then about regenerating the defensive line with speed and efficiency if possession is lost. An error at any stage of the defensive process will often result in a try for the opposition, so it is essential to develop a secure and organised defence.

Players are exposed in defence in sevens. One-on-one defence should be staple practice in the coaching programme, not only because it prepares players for a one-on-one situation in the game, but also because it enhances a player's competence and contribution when defending within the defensive line.

Tracking – concede line

Tracking is the term used to describe the line of approach to make a tackle, and will determine the success of the tackle itself. All defenders should move forwards to deny the attacking team time and space, but specifically they should advance from the *inside* of their opponents. If a defender positions directly in front of the ball carrier, his approach would have to be cautious to prepare for a break either side. Advancing from the inside gives the ball carrier only one direction in which to attack, allowing the defender to move up with more confidence and make a stronger tackle.

It is important to note that an inside approach does not mean that the defender allows the ball carrier to get far outside him, just that he advances in line with the attacker's inside shoulder, on an angle that forces the attacker to concede to running an outside line only. This is called the *concede line* in defence – closing off the possibility of an inside line and giving the ball carrier no option but to stay on an outside line. There is only a subtle difference in the angle of approach, but it is one that is very effective in narrowing the attacker's running options – see again figure 1.2 (page 17).

Tackle technique

A tackler should never be in a position where he has to reach out to tackle the ball carrier. Tacklers should be encouraged to lead with their head, and hit through the ball carrier. Leading with the head is important for reasons of safety, technique and overall tackle effectiveness. For safety, the tackler should keep his head in a neutral position and not lean away from the tackle. He should aim to push his head past the ball carrier and make solid contact with his outside shoulder. An outside shoulder hit reinforces good tracking from the inside.

Defenders should start with their inside foot forward and then use short quick

The idea of an imaginary hula-hoop around the feet of the ball carrier is a good way to teach novice players about correct foot positioning and range. The concept is simple but effective, and encourages the tackler to get his front foot inside the imaginary hoop just before contact is made. This enables him to stay balanced in the tackle and ensures he is close enough to make firm shoulder contact.

steps, not only to establish speed and momentum into contact but also to ensure the feet are close enough to the ball carrier so that initial contact is made with the shoulder and not the arms or hands. In general, players should understand that their feet will always follow their head, so if their head is correct in contact, they will make clean shoulder contact, and their feet will be right underneath to generate power into the tackle. The tackler should not plant his feet, but keep his feet active and running through the contact. Leading with the head is not easy for some players to grasp, but it sets up correct technique and, along with footwork, should be the focus in coaching tackle technique.

The shortening of the defender's stride just before contact should be combined with a late dip to achieve effective body height. On impact, the tackler should target the area just under the ball with his shoulder. Tackles around the legs are less effective in sevens as they allow the ball carrier to keep his arms free and offload the ball to a support runner. An offload allows a quick and fluid attack, and no time for the defence to reset or organise. The

Individual tackle technique

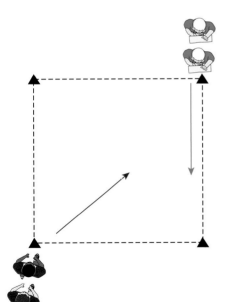

- The skill level of players determines the size of the grid; better players need a bigger grid.
- Players with tackle shields on one corner; tacklers on the diagonally opposite corner.
- Shield carriers simulate ball carriers and run straight.
- Defenders track, talk and tackle.
- Timed drill; after a set time, players change sides of the drill.
- Players then swap roles.

FIGURE 5.1

need to stop the ball moving must always be factored into the execution of the tackle. After driving the shoulder in just below the ball, the tackler then makes a decision, based on who has momentum in the tackle, whether to drive up to prevent the offload, or drive hard to ground to complete the tackle.

Defenders should wrap and squeeze their arms around the ball carrier to keep their shoulder pinned to the player and avoid falling off the tackle. Another option is to hook the leg of the ball carrier and lift it off the ground, which eliminates his power. The tackler should always keep his feet active in contact to try and drive the ball carrier backwards and further disrupt presentation or transfer of the ball. The focus is initially on stopping movement of the player and ball in every tackle, and then on regaining possession.

The defensive line

The defensive line is the basis of a sevens defensive structure. There is more detail than just keeping a level line of players across the field. Importantly, the defensive line should not spread out to cover the full width of the field all of the time, but remain close enough to stay

FIGURE 5.2
Defensive line: defenders should not be concerned if the attack position themselves wider than them. The priority is to stay connected.

connected as one unit, showing no clear opportunities for the attacking team, other than space on the outside.

There is no way around the idea that you have to play with a designated sweeper in defence. The old-fashioned pattern of using wingers to drop back as the ball moves away from them cannot be sustained for very long. There is also no way a player in the middle of the field can drop back during play because it would leave a hole in the defensive line. And without any sweeper at all, there would be no one to cover kicks and no last line of defence to slow down breaks. Good teams will, therefore, in most cases, choose to play with a sweeper.

With a sweeper behind, the defensive wall is made up of six players defending seven attackers, and so it must constantly shift and slide to cover the extra attacker. There is some advantage in a defence that has to keep sliding, as it is not immediately obvious to the attackers which defenders are marking them, and this makes it difficult to attack with purpose and precision.

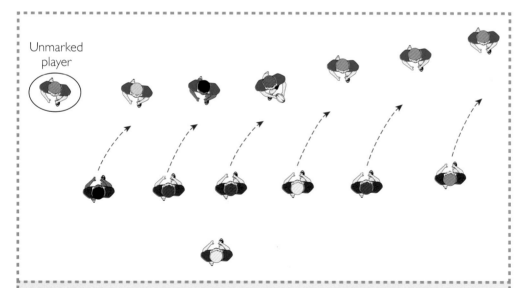

Unmarked player

FIGURE 5.3
Defenders move across the field as a line, numbering up from the outside and leaving the last attacker unmarked.

In order to cover the overlap, defenders must count from the *outside* inwards to identify and nominate the attacker they should be marking. Simply, the last defender covers the last attacker; the second last covers the second last attacker, and so on. This is called *numbering up* from the outside.

There will always be one player left unmarked on the attacking team, and the defence needs to ensure that it is the widest player in the opposite direction to where the ball is travelling. Defenders must be absolutely clear who they are marking at all times and communicate this to their teammates. Most importantly, there should always be a defender nominating

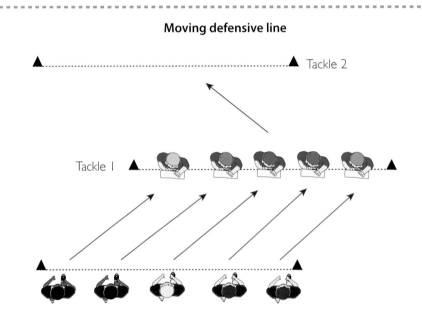

Moving defensive line

Tackle 2

Tackle 1

- 5 defenders form a defensive line between 2 cones
- 5 shield carriers line up opposite them.
- The defenders number up from the outside, identify their opponent, and hit the correct shield to simulate a tackle.
- After the tackle, the defenders perform a set number of press-ups (e.g. 3), while shield carriers reposition for Tackle 2.
- Defenders again slide across field to hit their pad.

FIGURE 5.4

the ball carrier. The sequence to teach is track – talk – tackle. That is (i) identify who you are marking, (ii) talk to your outside man (iii) go make a tackle! There is far too much hesitation in sevens defence, which just allows the attack to play. When defenders are encouraged to follow the sequence above and increase their tackle count, you have a defence that is successfully applying pressure instead of just sliding in front of the attack.

As the defenders track across the field to cover a wide attack, it is essential that they stay connected and keep an inside approach. As a rule, defenders must not advance *ahead* of the player on their *inside*, which happens when a player rushes out of the line to make a tackle. This severs the defensive line, isolates the defender and creates space for the attack. Players must understand the importance of defending as a team, not as individuals, specifically that they cannot move forward until the player on their inside moves forward too. To complement this, all defenders should work hard to get *ahead* of the player on their *outside*. This takes the line forward.

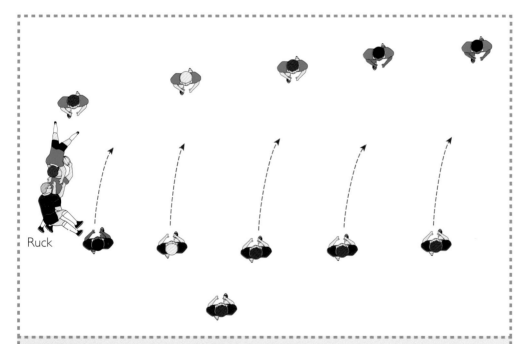

Ruck

FIGURE 5.5
The player nearest to the ruck should lead the line up. Importantly, the defensive line can only move forwards if it works together to do so.

The player nearest the source of attack – scrum, lineout, ruck, etc. – must initiate the process; he must move forward to get the whole line moving. If every defender knows that they must move forward in order to help others move forward, you create great teamwork, and a defensive line that is connected and applying pressure.

Inside cover

It is essential that every defender marking the ball carrier has inside cover. Inside cover is a form of insurance for the defender marking the ball carrier, protecting the space inside him from any attack, such as a side-step, switch or inside ball. As a defender moves across the field to cover his attacker, the player on his inside must slide simultaneously to close any gap that could open up between them. Inside cover must extend throughout the team and not just among the players immediately in front of the ball. Every defender must understand his responsibility to keep the line intact, even if he is a number of players away from the ball.

Simply, players should aim to keep equidistant from each other, right across the defensive line. This prevents any panic when the attack changes direction. The distance a defender keeps from the player outside him is down to his own judgement, but he must be close enough to safeguard against a side-step or inside pass, but not so close that the defensive

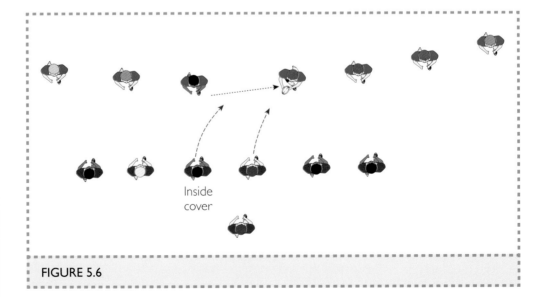

Inside
cover

FIGURE 5.6

line is overly compressed. Defenders must work together and aim to move smoothly as one unit rather than six individuals, connected by communication and a commitment to cover each other in the line. When called upon to make a tackle, the inside cover should be quick to kill the attack and give the defence a chance to reorganise.

Save

If a defender is unable to reach his opponent, the defender outside can save him. This means the outside defender leaves the player he is marking and comes in to make the tackle on the ball carrier. The decision to make this *save* can be called by the stretched defender himself, or by the outside defender. In defence, communication travels from inside to outside. If an outside defender does not hear his inside player nominating the ball carrier, there is obviously a problem. The defender who makes the save must change his angle very quickly to stun the attack and allow the ball carrier no time to react. He must also aim to make as aggressive a tackle as possible to prevent any offload and to give the defence a chance to reset their structure from the tackle. The practice of outside defenders coming in to make a tackle should generally be avoided in sevens as it breaks the pattern of an inside

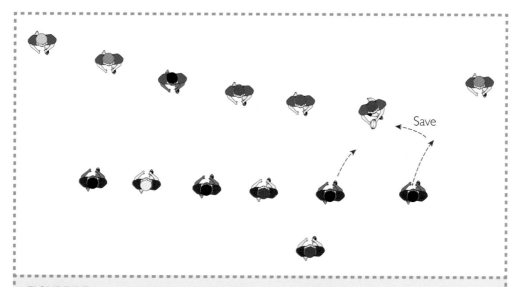

FIGURE 5.7
The player outside the defender marking the ball carrier changes his line of approach sharply to stun the attack.

approach and isolates the defender making the save, but it can be a useful play on a rare occasion to prevent a try.

Hinge defence

The only apparent way to beat a connected defensive line is to go around it, but space out wide should not worry a defence. It can be covered quickly with the correct running line and angle of approach. When the defence is stretched, defenders have to concede space to cover any overlap. In this situation, the defence cannot rush up on the attack, but must accurately number up on the attackers from the outside, and effectively cut off the try line from the attack.

1 v 3 / 2 v 3 / 3 v 3 Track defence

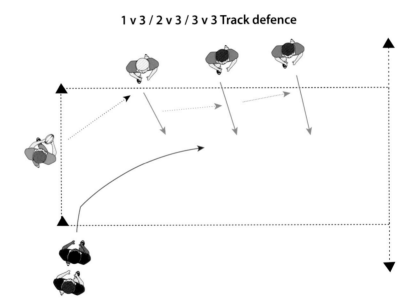

- Same set-up can be used for 2 v 3 and 3 v 3 to work a Hinge defence.
- The drill is best played from the middle of the field to a sideline.
- Attackers simply pass the ball to the wing, checking to see if the defender/s over-track. No attacking movement patterns allowed.
- The defender/s track and cover each attacker in turn.

FIGURE 5.8

Wide channels are easier to defend than the middle of the field because the touchline can be used to narrow the attackers' space. For this reason, the defence should aim to be particularly aggressive on a wide attack. When the opposition move the ball wide, the last defender should have total confidence to cover across at speed and trust his inside player to be there to cover him. Though he must do his best to maintain a controlled inside approach, he must also ensure that the attacker does not beat him on the outside. It is therefore essential that the last defender hears the support of a full and connected defensive line to prevent his opponent from getting around him. It should be considered the responsibility of the whole defensive team to prevent a break out wide, and not just the job of one defender.

The defence should seize the initiative when the ball moves wide, and use the concede line to trap the attackers and force them into contact. Specifically, the *hinge defence* happens on the *last* defender when the ball is in the *last* attacker's hands only. The last defender tracks on his opponent as usual, but the second-in defender moves up out of the line, to

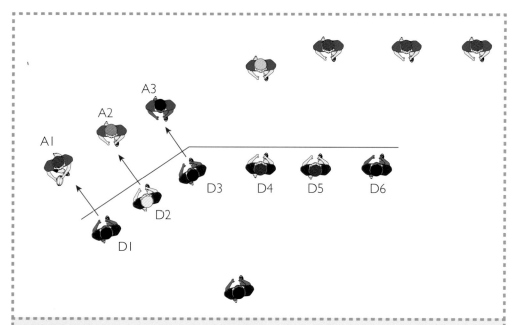

FIGURE 5.9

See the ramp-shape of the defence above; the defence hinges on the last defender (D1), and the second and third defenders (D2 and D3) push up on to the attack.

be quicker to make the tackle on his opponent (the second-in attacker) if an inside pass is made. Simultaneously, the third defender 'in' from the sideline does the same – he moves up on his opponent, to deter a deep inside pass.

If the last attacker (A1) throws an inside pass to A2, the second defender in (D2) is on the perfect line to make a dominant tackle, hitting his opponent while he is looking in the other direction to receive the ball. If the ball carrier (A1) decides to withdraw from contact and pass back deep to a support player (A3), the third defender in (D3) is also in a great position to hit his opponent as he receives the ball – ensuring another dominant tackle.

The other players in the defensive line importantly stay at the level of the *third-in* defender. If all of the defenders kept moving up on to their opponents, those furthest from the ball (D5 and D6) would have a long way to retreat to an offside line when contact is made. So, the principle is that the defenders *not* involved in the hinge (D4, D5, D6) stay at the level of the third-in defender, creating a ramp-shape in the defensive line as above.

The simple rule is, when the ball is wide, the defence can seize control, and force the attack into contact. The cue for the hinge is strictly when the ball is passed to the *last* attacker; only then do the defenders work the hinge, and move swiftly to shut down the attacking options. On contact, the defence has a chance to contest possession, or at least reset their defensive line, advantageously from a wide ruck with limited attacking options.

Sweeper

The sweeper plays an important role in ensuring the defensive line stays connected. He must be vocal and guide the defenders in front of him to prevent gaps from opening up in the defensive line. The sweeper is often the link player as he is best placed from set pieces to move into a sweeping position. Just as he does in attack, the sweeper generally maintains a position in the middle of the field, and tracks inside the ball behind the defensive line. The depth of his position will change on contact, and depend on whether the ball is in the middle of the field or out wide. If the ruck is around the centre of the field, the sweeper should move up closer to the defensive line, to better communicate with players and to plug holes if necessary around the tackle area. On a wide ruck, the easiest to defend, he can stay deeper, and monitor the situation from his central position. On wide rucks, his priority is

in communicating with players to reset the defensive line, equate numbers with the attack, and move off the line.

When a break is made, the sweeper should keep the ball carrier on his *outside* and use both the touchline and an inside track to narrow the attacker's space. He should also move forward to deny the ball carrier space and time to weigh up his options. A neat tactic is also to initially *concede* space, whilst keeping inside the ball, and then dynamically change the pace of his approach to upset the ball carrier's timing.

Choke tackle

Within the defensive line, defenders should communicate and cooperate in threes, with the player marking the ball carrier connected to the players on his inside and outside. Importantly, they do not operate in two designated three-player units like they do in the link structure. The threes in defence are constantly evolving as the attack moves the ball across the field – *three* is the player marking the ball, the player on his inside and the player on his outside. Communication boosts awareness, and ensures players mark the correct attacker for their position in the line. The player marking the ball carrier *must* nominate to prevent his outside defender coming in. Similarly, the player on the inside should always confirm he is in position – this gives the defender marking the ball carrier confidence to advance into the tackle.

Similarly, when contact is made, the inside and outside players should read the situation to decide whether or not they are needed to support the tackler. For example, they may choose to assist in the tackle if the ball carrier is still moving forward. In the first instance, only one support defender should commit to the tackle, and which one depends on the running line of the attack. If the ball carrier attacks outside the tackler, the *outside* defender should assist; and if he attacks the inside of the tackler, the *inside* defender assists. When either player chooses to commit to the tackle, it is vital that they wrap up the ball to prevent the ball carrier from offloading or playing it quickly.

More players can also commit to prevent the ball carrier from getting to ground. This is called a *choke tackle* and, when successful, effectively wins a scrum for the defending team. The defenders must weigh up the risk of this tactic and understand that if the attack manages to free the ball, the defence would be drastically short of numbers in the line.

Counter-ruck

The goal in defence is always to regain possession, and not just to prevent the attack from scoring. The nature of the tackle should dictate how defenders combine to win back the ball, with the principle being the first player possible targets the space beyond the tackled player and ball. For example, when a tackler makes a strong front-on tackle, he should use the momentum of his hit to immediately win the space *beyond* the ball, and leave the ball to be picked up by another defender. Whereas when a tackler is stretched and forced to make a side-on tackle, a support defender may be quicker to win this space over the ball.

When the tackler or other defender bends down to pick up the ball immediately following a tackle, he is often in a vulnerable position to be cleaned out easily by the speed and force of the attacking first support player. This has influenced the shift in priorities in turnover play. The counter-ruck is no longer a race to get hands on the ball, but a race to win the space *beyond* the ball. Obviously, if the ball carrier is isolated from support, the tackler should target the ball, but the principle should always be to get a player beyond the ball *first* – sometimes this will be the tackler; sometimes it will be the arriving defender.

A defender driving past the ball at the ruck presents a new challenge for the attack, which will be used to defenders conventionally reaching over the tackled player to get the ball. Defenders who go straight for the ball are easy targets; defenders who drive past the ball present the attack with an unfamiliar target and a player in balance to withstand a contest.

> Defenders should mentally treat the ruck like it is their own – that is, they hit the ruck with a clear purpose to win the ball, and this is only achieved by claiming the space beyond the ball and the tackled player. The trigger is the ball hitting the ground. As soon as the ball is on the floor, it becomes a race to the space over the ball – the team that wins this race will most often win the ball (in attack *and* defence).

When the counter-ruck is successful, the tackled player is effectively isolated with the ball. Periphery defenders should be reading the situation, and be quick to react and collect the ball when it is available. The sweeper, who positions flatter on rucks in the middle of the field, is also in a great position to manage the situation and play the ball when it is won.

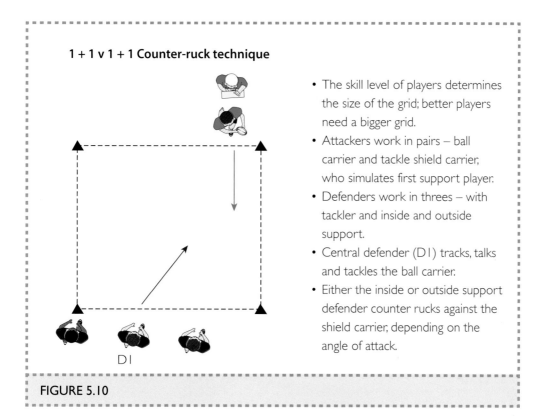

1 + 1 v 1 + 1 Counter-ruck technique

- The skill level of players determines the size of the grid; better players need a bigger grid.
- Attackers work in pairs – ball carrier and tackle shield carrier, who simulates first support player.
- Defenders work in threes – with tackler and inside and outside support.
- Central defender (D1) tracks, talks and tackles the ball carrier.
- Either the inside or outside support defender counter rucks against the shield carrier, depending on the angle of attack.

D1

FIGURE 5.10

Even when possession is not won, an aggressive counter-ruck is usually sufficient to slow down the delivery of the ball in the ruck, and allow adequate time for the defenders to organise and reset their defensive line. Importantly, the support defender must stay on his feet whether he assists in the tackle or contests possession. Indeed, there should never be more than one defender on the floor – that is, the tackler – and he should always aim to get back to his feet as quickly as possible. When the counter-rucking defender accepts that the ball is lost, or when he is driven back from the tackle contest, he should take up a position just behind the ruck, on guard for a run from the attacking halfback. Once the halfback passes, he quickly moves into the defensive line and offers inside cover to the defender marking the first receiver.

A neat tactic, when the attacking first support player is *bridging* over the ball at the ruck, is to initially pause contesting for the ball, and then drive the bridging player back just as the halfback is picking it up. This can work to disrupt his handling and force a knock-on. Another option is to pull the bridging player *through* to release the ball from the ruck. The defender must always weigh up his chances of success before committing to the tackle contest because, at times, it may be a better option to let the opposition have the ball, and prioritise setting the defensive line.

Post-tackle work rate

A ruck effectively destroys a defensive line. It is an unavoidable irony of sevens defence – you make tackles, which create rucks, which in turn give you big headaches. One minute you are moving as one connected line of six players (with a sweeper at the back), the next minute you are scrambling to deal with a big obstacle that has severed the defensive line.

Every time there is a tackle, defenders have to reposition as they reorganise the defensive line. They have to consider offside lines, assess where the attack is likely to strike next, and nominate whom they are marking. The most important thing following a tackle is that the defenders are able to match the number of attackers either side of the ruck. It is essential that defenders are aggressive and accurate in their counter-ruck, to force the attack to commit three players to the tackle situation, which then gives the defence the chance to equate numbers exactly. Three attackers at the ruck leaves four attackers in the field.

The defence should actively compress following a tackle to facilitate communication and to stop an immediate break around the ruck, but then be quick to reload to a position just inside their opponent. The principles of the defensive line should be reapplied – that is, the

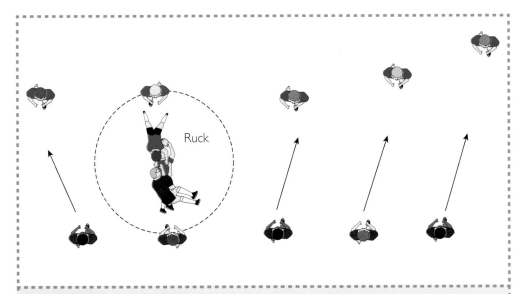

Ruck

FIGURE 5.11
Players must communicate and show urgency to equate numbers either side of the ruck.

last defender marks the last attacker, and so on. Where possible the tackler should get to his feet and take up a position directly behind the ruck, on guard for an attack to either side by the opposing halfback. If the tackler is caught on the ground, another player must take up this position, and be quick to move into the defensive line when the halfback passes the ball. In particular, the player behind the ruck has to provide urgent inside cover to the defender marking the first attacker.

Players should use every breakdown as an opportunity to reset their defensive line, and this offers an achievable framework for defence. Players should also understand that their urgency, communication and work rate must increase, and not decrease, at ruck time. Rucks are not a time to rest!

There are two good defensive calls which encourage team communication, help coordinate line speed and raise overall awareness of a situation – *hover* and *sting*. When the defence is outnumbered, players call 'Hover', which is an indication that they need to slide in defence to cover the overlap and equate numbers. Alternatively, when the defence has equal numbers with the attack, say following a ruck, they call 'Sting', which is a signal to move up quickly on the attack. Teams should minimise the *hover* in their defence as much as possible, always aiming to equate numbers and reload to a position just inside their opponent. Defence is about *applying* pressure, not absorbing it, and players should understand that going forward is as much an aim in defence as it is in attack.

Finally, defenders should be confident and relaxed in their structure, and avoid any panic that could cause a disconnection or error in the line. A relaxed state of mind happens with trust, raised awareness, and after repetitive and disciplined practice. This helps players become immune to the pressure of defending in the wide open spaces of a sevens field. See again the drill illustrated in figure 3.1 (page 44).

Scrum defence

Scrum defence is first about contesting possession, and then establishing the defensive line to cover any immediate attacking threats.

The forwards should aim to drive their opponents off the ball in the first instance, but would be wise to weigh up their chances of success with this option. There is a good possibility that by committing fully to the drive, players will be slower to break from the scrum, which could leave the team defensively exposed if the attack strikes quickly. Fundamentally, the defence should compete aggressively enough on engagement to force an uncontrolled delivery of the ball, which can be immediately contested by the halfback. The law does not allow the ball to be kicked out of the scrum in the direction of the opponent's goal line.

The hooker is a key player in establishing the defensive line from a scrum. His movement from the scrum is determined by where it is on the field and the anticipated attack. On the right side of the field, the hooker breaks left and runs to cover the inside of the defending fly half, connecting forwards and backs as one defensive line. The halfback hustles his opponent for the ball, covers any attack to the right of the scrum, and then drops back to sweep.

Scrums in sevens are generally scrappy contests, so the defending halfback often has an opportunity to pounce on the ball as it is released from the scrum, or at least a good chance of tackling the opposing halfback as he picks up the ball.

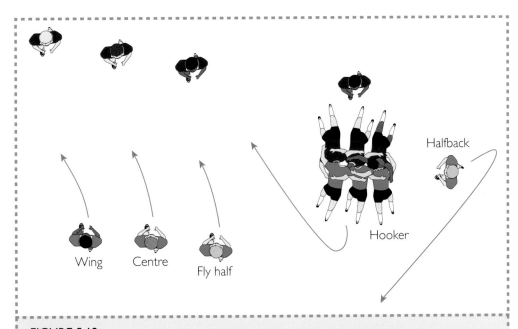

Halfback

Hooker

Wing   Centre

Fly half

FIGURE 5.12
Right-field scrum defence: the hooker breaks left.

Backline defence from a scrum is all about running the defensive pattern. It is important that they move up quickly but not erratically, so that their approach is controlled. On a right field scrum, the fly half must stay alert for a break from the attacking halfback before advancing on his opposite player. It is the hooker's responsibility to let the fly half know as soon as he is in the line, so that the fly half can move up with confidence to cover his own player.

From a scrum on the left side of the field, the halfback and hooker must communicate to determine who will cover the left side of the scrum. If the opposition halfback poses an attacking threat, the worry is that the hooker will not be able to break from the scrum in time to cover him. In this case, the defending halfback should position directly behind the scrum to cover any attack to the left. The hooker then breaks to the right side of the scrum and takes up a place in the defensive line, inside the fly half, as he did from the scrum on the right side of the field. If the defence wants to prioritise pressure on the opposing halfback, and is confident that the hooker can break from the scrum quickly enough, then the halfback can stay and challenge his opponent at the base of the scrum. However, as a general rule, the defending hooker breaks to the open[9] side of the scrum, and consistently takes up a position in the defensive line inside the fly half.

For midfield scrums, or where the attack has split its players either side of the scrum, the hooker and halfback assess the situation and communicate to determine which side the hooker will break from the scrum. The defending backline players should simply match their opponents. The rule is, when the halfback *pressurises* his opponent, the hooker breaks *left*; when the halfback positions *behind* the scrum, the hooker breaks *right*. Simple.

Lineout defence

There are very few lineouts in sevens, but defending players must still be given clear and defined roles for this component of the game. Like the scrum, lineout defence is about achieving a balance between contesting possession and establishing the defensive line.

Committing three players to the jump – a jumper and two lifters – provides the sternest challenge for the ball in defence.

[9]The open side of the scrum is the side of the scrum towards the middle of the field.

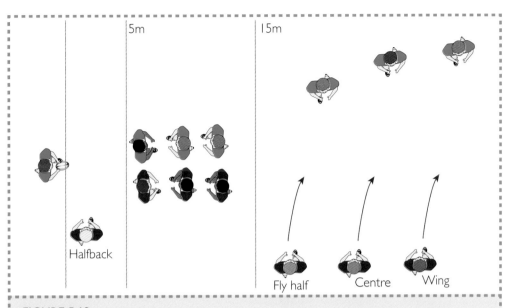

FIGURE 5.13
The forwards contest possession and all players mark up on their opposite number.

Speed is a key factor in lineout success. If the attacking and defending teams jump directly against each other, the team that is quickest in the air will win the ball. In most cases, the attacking team will use movement before the ball is thrown to find space and gain an advantage. If the attacking jumper runs forward to be lifted, the defence should follow and try to beat their opponents to the ball in the air. If the attackers then, or even initially, run backwards, the defence should, as a general rule, hold their position and just aim for as high a jump as possible to pressure the throw. Importantly, the defending jumper should watch the thrower carefully to time his jump. In defence, watching the thrower and anticipating the throw will produce more turnovers at the lineout than the conventional practice of trying to exactly mirror the movement of the opposition jumper.

The drawback of committing three players to the jump is the lack of cover for the overthrow. The defence must have a player standing between the touchline and the 5-metre line, so the only option, in order to commit three players to the jump *and* cover the overthrow, is to move a player from the backline to the back of the lineout, specifically to a position at the back of the lineout and two metres from the line of touch[10] as the law demands.

[10]The line of touch is an imaginary line running through the very middle of the lineout.

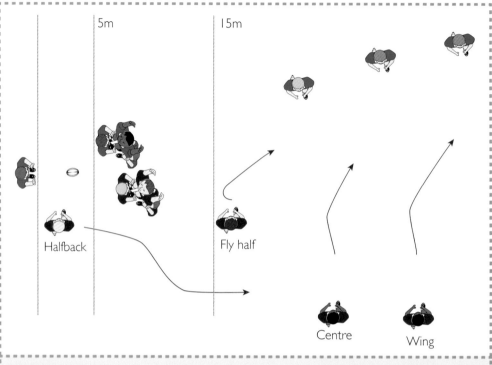

5m 15m

Halfback

Fly half

Centre

Wing

FIGURE 5.14
To contest the throw with three players *and* cover the overthrow, the fly half can move to the back of the lineout.

This positioning puts maximum pressure on the throw and jump, but compromises the width of the defensive alignment. It is not as radical as it seems because the defending fly half is actually not much further from his opponent than he would usually be – he just approaches from a different angle. In this situation, it would be advantageous for the halfback to initially track inside the fly half to provide the necessary inside cover for his line of approach.

The alternative to all three defending forwards being involved in the jump is a *one-man lift*. A one-man lift is a difficult but ideal technique in defending the lineout. One defender simply lifts another, allowing the third forward to stand at the back of the lineout (two metres from the line of touch), and commit to the defensive line instead of the lift.

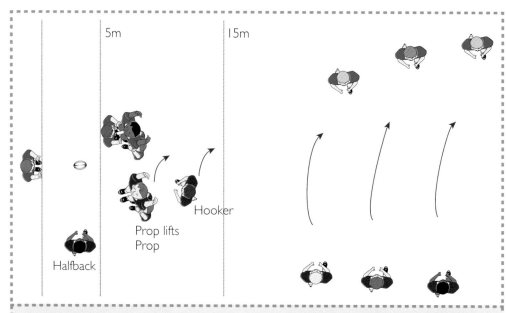

5m   15m

Hooker

Prop lifts
Prop

Halfback

FIGURE 5.15

In this example, the hooker positions at the back of the lineout and is quick to push into the defensive line. The halfback stands in the 5m channel then sweeps.

The one-man lift is effective in creating enough of a contest in the air to disrupt the opposition or force an overthrow. The defender at the back of the lineout is perfectly positioned to catch an overthrow, *and* deter the attacking halfback from running around the back of the lineout. This set-up also allows the defence to match the width of the attacking alignment and move up quickly on its opponents with better inside cover. It is most advantageous for the hooker to play at the back of the lineout, to keep his familiar role of linking up with the fly half in the defensive line. The one-man lift prioritises the defensive line over contesting the primary possession.

Defenders in the lineout have a tendency to slide too quickly when the lineout ends, which leaves the defence vulnerable to a change of direction. Players in the lineout should be encouraged to move forward first, and then across, as they form the defensive line, and be prepared for a sudden attack back towards their side of the field. As ever, they should quickly determine where they stand in the defensive line and identify which attacker they are marking by numbering up from the outside.

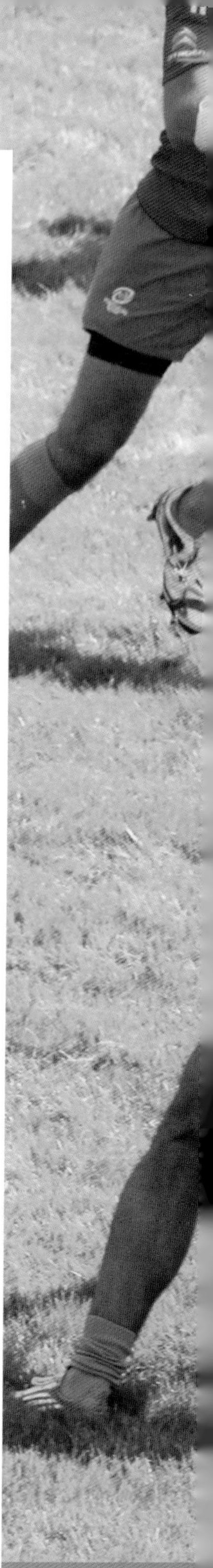

LESSON 5: PLAY WITH DISCIPLINE

Checklist

- [ ] Tracking
- [ ] Concede line
- [ ] Tackle technique
- [ ] The defensive line
- [ ] Staying connected
- [ ] Don't get ahead of your inside man
- [ ] Inside cover
- [ ] Save
- [ ] Hinge defence
- [ ] Sweeper
- [ ] Counter-ruck
- [ ] Post-tackle work-rate
- [ ] Hover and sting
- [ ] Scrum defence
- [ ] Lineout defence
- [ ] One-man lift

6

WORK ON YOUR RESTARTS

Primary possession is key to maintaining momentum in rugby, both in sevens and fifteens. This mainly refers to winning your own ball in scrums, lineouts, free kicks and kick offs.

A starter play is a rehearsed movement pattern from a scrum, lineout, free kick or penalty. A starter play should aim to beat the defence with a direct attacking play. Most of the attacking movement patterns, linked with the secondary support plays, are ideal for starter plays, but more complex plays can be used from a set piece as players have more time to plan and communicate.

The choice of starter play is determined by the set piece – bearing in mind offside lines – by field position and by how we know defenders will move and respond to the situation. It is worth keeping an open mind about the application of the suggested starter plays; for example, a move suggested for a right field scrum *can* work off a left-field scrum, and the scrum plays *can* work off lineouts and vice versa. The illustrations are also a useful guide for positioning of both attackers and defenders at set piece time.

The scrum

There are a few considerations at the scrum to ensure the attacking team retains the ball. Players should establish a stable base with their feet, slightly over shoulder-width apart, and achieve a safe body position with shoulders above hips. Props should have their outside foot slightly ahead of their inside foot. When the ball is put in the scrum, props should aim to step forward with their inside foot, to deliver a ball that is further away and more difficult for the opposing halfback to contest.

There are a couple of options for binding, namely an *over-bind* which is roughly comparable to how front row players bind in a 15-a-side game, where the hooker's armpits sit on top of the props' shoulders; and an *under-bind*, where the hooker binds underneath the arms of the props, with the top of his shoulders in the armpits of the props.

The advantage of the *under-bind* is that the hooker can get away from the scrum and enter the attack quickly. While the *under-bind* is certainly the preferred method for most teams, it positions the hooker a little further away from the ball and effectively leaves the two props to control and stabilise the scrum, which could cause problems against strong opposition. The advantage of the *over-bind* is that it makes for a more stable unit and, therefore, a more solid platform to secure and release the ball; but the hooker may be slightly slower to leave the scrum. Players should be aware of both methods of binding and consider the situation and strengths of the opposition before making their decision.

It is best to give the opposition as little time as possible to settle, contest or disrupt the scrum, so the halfback should put the ball into the scrum immediately upon engagement. Players should squat quite low before engagement and drive up and forwards into their opposition. They should aim to step over the ball in unison rather than the hooker performing a conventional strike at the ball. The movement of front row players should be explosive, accurate and coordinated, so the ball is in, out, and away from the scrum very quickly.

> Attacking props can easily delay their opponents' exit from the scrum with their binding and overall intensity of their contest. This can give the attack an advantage, leaving areas of the field undefended momentarily and open to be exploited by the starter play.

Good players will continue to work on the ground until the halfback has the ball in his hands.

SCRUM STARTER PLAYS

The width of the attacking alignment at scrum time is determined and often limited by the position of the defending halfback. Because the scrum in sevens comprises just a front row, the defending halfback can be quick to pounce on the ball or his opponent when the ball emerges from the scrum. This pressure will obviously affect the accuracy and predictability of the attacking halfback's clearing pass.

The defending halfback must stand on the same side of the scrum as the attacking halfback, or behind the offside line defined for other players, that is, five metres from the scrum. Since the attacking halfback conventionally throws the ball into the *left* side of the scrum, his pass is under less pressure on left-field scrums than on right-field scrums. This is because his opponent is behind him on left-field scrums and away from the target area of attack; but on right field scrums, the defending halfback is directly in the passing channel to the fly half.

However, the law does not stipulate in which side of the scrum the halfback must throw the ball so, on right field scrums, he *can* choose to put the ball into the *right* of the scrum, instead of the left. This pulls the defending halfback to the right, and away from the target area of attack, making for an easier pass and allowing the attacking fly half to position slightly wider. He can also stand wider when the defending halfback chooses not to contest the ball at all, and positions behind the scrum.

In general, the fly half should prioritise possession over width, and be prepared to stand almost directly behind the scrum where his halfback is under severe pressure. Better to have the ball than not.

Right-field scrum starter 1

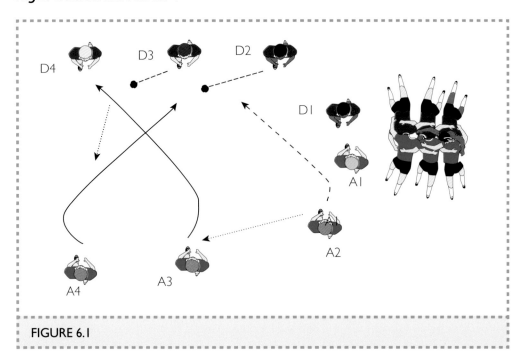

FIGURE 6.1

Figure 6.1 shows the attacking halfback (A1) putting in the ball on the conventional left side of the scrum. The play is simply a 'stay-out' between the centre (A3) and wing (A4), with the fly half (A2) running a secondary support play of short or doubles. The centre must aim to beat his opponent (D3) to set up the play. Refer to the attacking movement patterns in Lesson 1 and secondary support plays in Lesson 3.

Right-field scrum starter 2

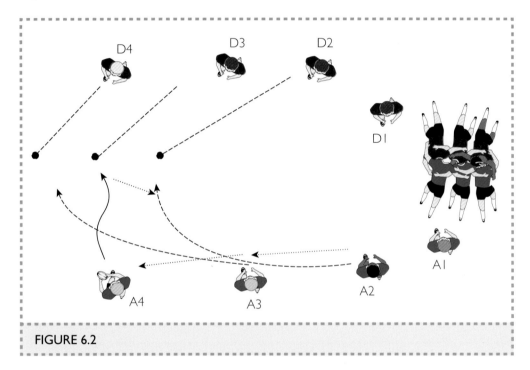

FIGURE 6.2

This starter play is effectively a planned 'run-round-me' on the wing (A4). There are numerous options that can be run to great effect off this movement pattern. The key is to get the ball to the wing as soon as possible, and for the centre (A3) to wrap as far outside the wing as possible to stretch the defence. The wing should look to sell the outside runner to the defence, by looking and shaping to pass to the *outside*. Once the movement is complete, the wing can either (i) pass outside; (ii) run himself; (iii) play a 'you-and-me' with the fly half (A2); or (iv) just fake the pass and run behind the inside runner to space.

Left-field scrum starter 1

A left-field scrum is a great attacking platform because the defending halfback is on the far side of the scrum from the attack, which makes the defenders in the backline exposed and vulnerable to one-on-ones. This starter play is effectively a 'put-away' between fly half (A2) and centre (A3). The centre must step inside dynamically to stretch his opponent and keep his arms free in the tackle. The fly half must be patient and wait for the centre to step in before running to the outside. The acceleration and coordination in this attacking movement pattern gives the defence no time to adjust.

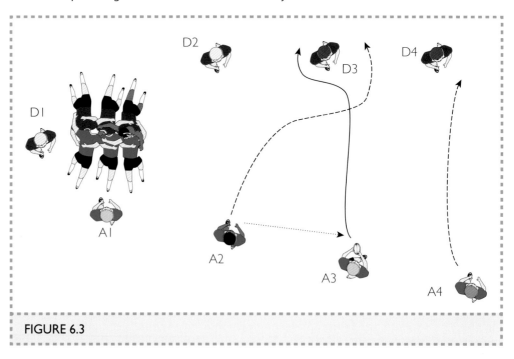

FIGURE 6.3

Left-field scrum starter 2

This is a simple 'short-ball' between the fly half (A2) and centre (A3), which turns into a 'stay-out' between fly half and wing (A4). Even though the plan is always to give the wrap pass, the centre must still aim to *beat* the defence with his running line. A well-timed angle change will either put him through the defensive line or at least turn his opponent away from the intended area of attack. The fly half's wrap sets him on an effective running line for a 'stay-out' with the wing.

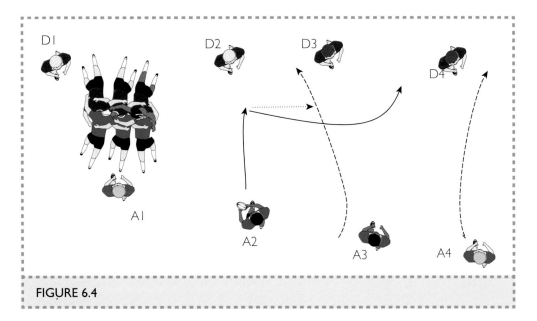

FIGURE 6.4

Split-field scrum starter

A split-field scrum is when the attackers split their backline either side of the scrum. This will affect the make-up of the attacking units after the scrum, with forwards and backs mixed, but players should just work towards the principle of supporting in threes and setting a link

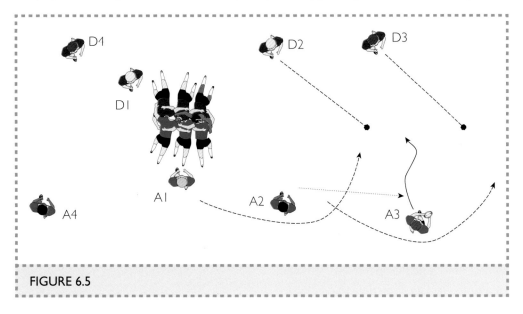

FIGURE 6.5

player in position to establish the link structure. As a general principle, the halfback follows his pass and joins the attack to create a 3-player attacking unit. The hooker, first to break from the scrum, fills the link role. The value of the split-field scrum is that it sets up a 2 v 2 on one side of the field, which is the perfect platform for all of the attacking movement patterns.

The example above shows a variation of the 'run-round-me', but other attacking movement patterns could be just as effective. The backs adopt a split formation, with the wing (A2) and the centre (A3) on the right of the scrum, and the fly half (A4) alone on the left side. The halfback (A1) passes to the wing (A2) and follows his pass. The wing passes to the centre (A3) and runs around him as fast as possible to force the defenders to slide across at pace. The attacking halfback (A1) runs an inside line off the centre (A3), who *sells* the outside to the defence, and then plays a 'you-and-me' with the halfback. The halfback may find that he can break the line without the need to pass back for the 'you-and-me'. This move tests how quickly the defending props can break from the scrum and provide inside cover. The attacking props can contribute by trying to delay their opponents' exit from the scrum.

The lineout

Though there are few lineouts in a game of sevens, they must still be practised to make sure a team never loses the ball on its own throw. The player that throws the ball into the lineout is also the player who receives it back from the jumper to clear the ball to the backline. The halfback is most often selected to throw the ball, since he is the player in the team with the best clearing pass. The lineout does not need to be very complicated. For example, if the defence is not competing for the ball in the air, then a very basic move will often be enough to secure possession.

In Option 1, the three forwards set up for a basic jump and lift. As the ball leaves the thrower's hands, the lifters support the jumper to meet the ball in the air. The jumper should aim to reach his hands in front of those of his opponent if there is a late contest. This basic set-up remains consistent for all lineouts, but if the defending players

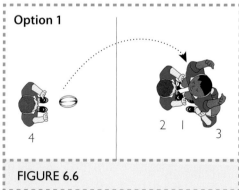

Option 1

FIGURE 6.6

look poised to jump, the attacking team can use movement to beat their opponents. It is important that the general principle of attack – of beating the opposition to space – is not overlooked in coaching the lineout.

In Option 2, the front lifter stays facing the throw, prior to any lift. If his opponent does not mark him, the halfback simply executes a straight and low throw for the front lifter to catch. The two players combine quickly, to get the ball back in the halfback's hands to clear the ball. If the front lifter's opponent follows him, it is the front lifter who sets the timing and chooses when to turn sharply, racing his opposite number back to the lift. If you and I had a race, and I said 'Go', I am pretty sure I would beat you over the first five metres!

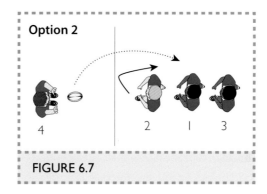

FIGURE 6.7

Option 3 is a variation on Option 2. The front lifter approaches the jumper to lift. If his opponent follows, he runs to the front of the lineout to receive a quick and low throw from the halfback.

The jumper and back lifter should also compress towards the front of the lineout. This effectively shields the halfback when he receives the ball back from the front lifter, or provides a get-out option for the front lifter. If his opponent chases and manages to cover him, the front lifter can simply turn and meet the jumper for a supported jump at the ball.

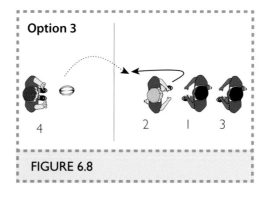

FIGURE 6.8

Option 4 is a variation on option 3, where the *jumper* runs to the front from his position between the two lifters, but again, only when he sees that the defence is committed to the lift. The jumper's movement must be dynamic to beat the defence. At the same time, the back lifter should drift to the very back of the lineout, to give the thrower an option to throw the ball over the defence. In this case, the front lifter also peels around the back of the lineout to take a pass from the back lifter. Option 4 wins the ball with movement alone and no jump or lift.

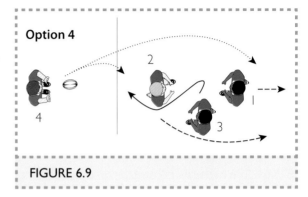

FIGURE 6.9

In most lineouts, the ball is most often returned to the halfback off the top of the jump; that is, while the jumper is still in the air. This sets the attack underway quickly, but also allows the defence, particularly the defender at the back of the lineout, to start advancing and applying pressure just as quickly. For this reason, the halfback should use a call to signal if he wants the jumper to *land* before giving him the ball. The defence then has to check its run and stay onside, which relieves pressure on the attacking fly half.

The action of landing to deliver the ball can be used as a set play, especially for a lineout close to the opposition try line. In Option 5, the jumper lands with the ball and turns as usual towards his halfback. Instead of giving the ball as expected to the halfback, he fakes the pass and spins round and drives for the try line, powered by his support players.

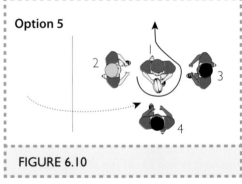

FIGURE 6.10

In sevens, defenders rarely anticipate a drive from the lineout, so Option 5 can be a worthwhile and often try-scoring tactic close to the line. The worst that can happen is that the ball carrier will be tackled with two support players right alongside him!

LINEOUT STARTER PLAYS

The main consideration for lineout starter plays is the additional depth of the offside lines compared to scrums. It should be remembered that rather than just giving the attack more space and time on the ball, it also gives the defence more time and space to read and adjust to the attack.

The assumption is that the defence will use all three players in the lineout to contest the ball in the air. If it doesn't, then the attack will need to consider the defender at the back of the lineout who can break from the lineout very quickly. On this occasion, the halfback should instruct the jumper to *land* with the ball, to check the defender's advance.

Lineout starter 1

This is simply a 'stay-out' between centre (A3) and wing (A4), with a doubles secondary support play. It is effectively a double switch, but it is important for timing that the players run it like a 'stay-out' and doubles. In fact, the attackers should aim to beat the defence at every stage of the play. The centre (A3) should work hard to reload after giving his switch pass, to set up a 2 v 1 against the opposition wing (D4) when the fly half (A2) runs the doubles.

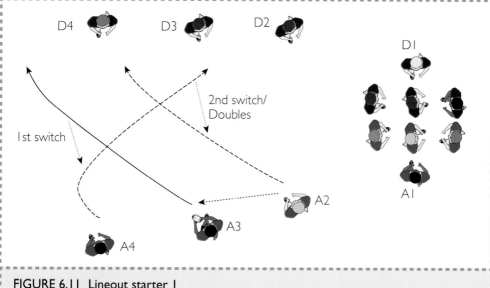

FIGURE 6.11 Lineout starter 1

Lineout starter 2

This starter play is a modified 'run-round-me', with a doubles. The halfback (A1) runs off the back of the lineout to facilitate a pass straight to the centre (A3), missing out the fly half. As the ball is passed in front of him, the fly half (A2) loops around the centre. The halfback follows his pass and also wraps around the centre, receiving a pass back on the inside. The play creates at least a 3 v 2 on the outside, but if the centre manages to fix his opponent (D3) with the strength and angle of his running line, it is possible to create a 3 v 1.

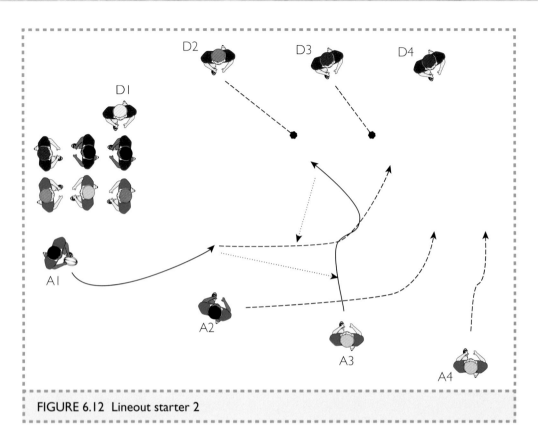

FIGURE 6.12 Lineout starter 2

Lineout starter 3

This play takes advantage of the momentum of the halfback's running line off the lineout, and exploits the opposition contesting the lineout ball with all three forwards. The halfback (A1) hits top speed and targets the defending fly half (D2). If the fly half stays out to cover the attacking fly half (A2), he will leave a gap for the halfback, so he *must* hold, which then creates an overlap outside. The play is best when all players in the backline are in motion – if the wing is running straight, he attracts the attention of his opponent, drawing him from the unmarked centre. Success of the play is determined by the speed of the halfback and his ability to threaten the defending fly half; everything else falls into place. If the centre is tackled, the wing should hold a wide position to create a valuable 3-1 split field for the halfback to exploit from the ruck (See Situational play in Lesson 3, page 51–56).

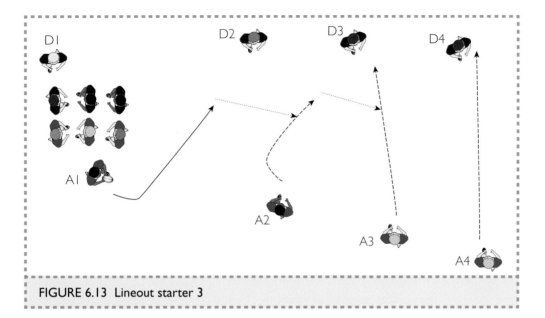

FIGURE 6.13 Lineout starter 3

Free kicks

Whilst there are fewer set pieces in sevens than in fifteens, especially lineouts, there are generally more free kicks and penalties (in such a concentrated period of time) due to the transparency of the tackle area.

FREE KICK STARTER PLAYS

Taking the right option at a penalty can mean the difference between winning and losing, and a split-second decision is often needed to seize the initiative. Players should show both urgency and composure to take advantage of any scoring opportunity. Various factors influence the decision, such as field position, the score line, time left in the game, and the state of the defence. The options from a penalty are to take a quick tap, run a set move, or kick for touch or goal. From free kicks, the options are limited to a quick tap or set moves. A quick tap is often the preferred choice from penalties or free kicks as it presents an opportunity to run against a disorganised and retreating defence. A common problem, however, is that the ball carrier darts off and isolates himself from support, nullifying the advantage of the penalty. The expectation should be for support to keep up with the ball carrier, and not for the ball carrier to slow down for support, so support players must aim to react simultaneously when a penalty is awarded and immediately start communicating with the ball carrier and directing play. The attacking movement patterns are particularly effective from a quick tap.

Set moves can be used anywhere on the field, but are most deadly in the opposition half and close to the opposition try line. Their design is based on manipulating the movement of the defence to create a scoring opportunity. A good defence should close the attack down very quickly to disrupt their timing, yet teams defending set penalty moves often adopt a much more cautious approach. The defensive line may be well organised, but it often advances with little conviction which gives the attack more time and space to complete the planned movement of the set play.

Importantly, the set moves should be seen as an initial framework to shift and open the defence. Players then have to keep assessing the state of the defence and make decisions. The set moves are notably based on the attacking movement patterns, so the considerable time spent on these in the coaching programme also benefits the development of set penalty moves.

Set move 1

Set move 1 is specifically for penalties or free kicks around the middle of the field, and works on the principle of moving defenders to create space to attack.

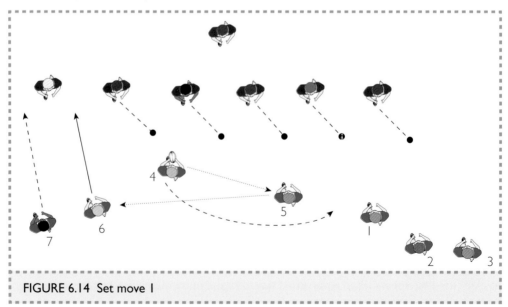

FIGURE 6.14 Set move 1

Set move 1 aims to create a clear 2 v 1 situation as quickly as possible. The move specifically exploits the six-man defensive line where the last attacker is left unmarked. The halfback (4) makes a pass to the fly half (5) and loops around him, forcing the defence to slide across to cover. If the defence number up exactly, the fly half (5) should make a long flat pass back to the two players (6 and 7) on the other side of the field, to execute a 2 v 1 on the last defender. If the defence does not slide, then the fly half has the option to use the overlap created by the halfback's loop.

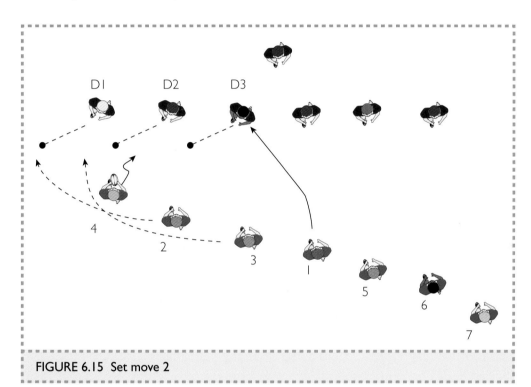

FIGURE 6.15 Set move 2

Set move 2

Set move 2 is designed for a penalty or free kick on the left- or right-hand side of the field. The attacking movement tests the *inside cover* of the defence, and again exploits the fact that defences number up from the outside.

Players align as illustrated above. The halfback (4) on the ball, the three forwards outside him, then the backline unit outside them. The movement begins when the halfback places the ball on the ground, which is the signal for the two forwards outside him (2 and 3) to run around him as fast as possible. It is not difficult for defenders to cover these two players, but their movement serves to stretch the defence and open up gaps. As on a 'run-round-me', the halfback (4) should *sell* the outside to the defence by looking, shaping to pass and even running towards the looping players. He should then change direction suddenly, to fix his marker (D3). The halfback then plays a 'short-ball' to the third forward (1) who has timed an angled run and, if necessary, can return the pass to the halfback on the wrap. Either he will go straight through the defence, or the halfback will break the line after the wrap.

Set move 3

This is another set move for penalties or free kicks awarded around the middle of the field, and works on the principle of moving defenders to create space to attack.

The play is a simple 'you-and-me' between the halfback and a powerful running forward positioned on his inside (1). The alignment of players in these positions facilitates the link structure after the movement is complete, with backs together and forwards together. The move is started with a long pass from the fly half to the halfback. The halfback runs an

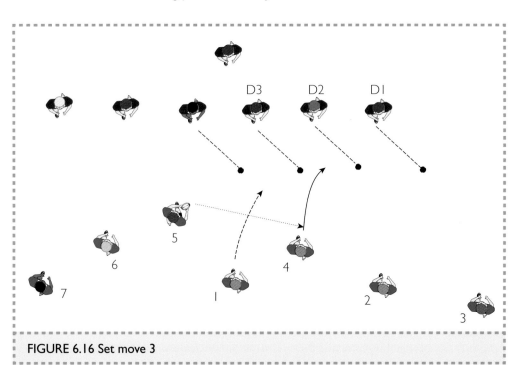

FIGURE 6.16 Set move 3

outside line to try to beat his marker (D3), setting up the 'you-and-me' with the forward on his inside. When the halfback wraps the inside pass, he will find himself in space, or at least with a significant overlap on the other side of the field.

Kick offs

Given the sevens law variation – that the scoring team kicks off – kick restarts need to feature consistently in the coaching programme. And depending on how good your team is at scoring tries, you will need to practise both chasing and receiving kick offs.

KICKING TEAM

There are two main options at kick off – high kick short on the 10-metre line or high kick long down the 15-metre channel. The consistent factor is the height of the kick, which gives the chasers the best chance to contest for the ball in the air. The option of a short grubber kick just over the 10-metre line can be taken if the opposition is out of position. This is usually a spontaneous decision made by the kicker rather than a planned tactic.

The kick must be accurate, whether short or long. This takes intensive practice, but the main piece of advice to give to the kicker is to 'watch your foot strike the ball'. It is as straightforward as it sounds, but it is a fact that most poor kicks are a result of the kicker failing to keep his eye on the ball at that crucial moment when boot strikes ball. He should also drop the ball on its end from a point no higher than his knee to be sure of a controlled drop and adequate bounce. Then it is down to practice and developing a personal system that can be repeated with consistent success.

The kick is notably only as good as the chase, and players need to develop clarity of roles and responsibilities when chasing kick offs. Because most kickers are right-footed, most kick offs are kicked to the left side of the field. Bear in mind, a kick to the left demands that chasing players have to turn to compete for the ball with their *left* arm, and a kick to the right facilitates chasers turning to catch the ball with their favoured right arm. This is worth considering once the accuracy of the kick is guaranteed.

Short kick off

Option 1 is an aggressive chasing pattern, which applies maximum pressure on the opposition, and sets the players in a connected defensive alignment if the ball is lost. All

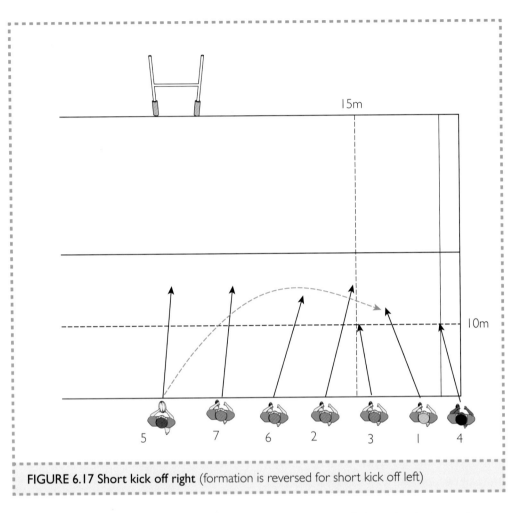

FIGURE 6.17 Short kick off right (formation is reversed for short kick off left)

of the players have specific roles in the pattern. The Props (1 and 3) are the designated jumpers whose aim is to contest the ball in the air, chasing the kick from the outside so they can keep sight of the ball throughout their approach. It is essential that these two players communicate on the run to decide who is best positioned to go up for the catch. If it is a good kick, one of them should jump for it, and the other should slow his approach and fall in directly behind the jump to field a tap back. If it is a poor kick, neither may jump, instead choosing to target and tackle the opposition catcher and work for the turnover.

The hooker (2) advances *beyond* the ball to intercept any tap back between the opposition catcher and his support. The halfback (4) moves forward to cover any immediate attacks to the blind side, and is in a safe position to retreat to his sweeping role. He is also close enough to contribute to the attack if the ball is won in the air. The backline players – 5, 6 and 7 – are integral in establishing the defensive line, and applying pressure in midfield. They should advance quickly to cut off a long pass infield, and force the opposition into contact.

Long kick off

The set-up for a long kick off is similar to the short kick off, with chasers spread slightly wider to prepare for the receiving team moving the ball quickly from the catch.

All players push up in a defensive line except the halfback who holds a deep position to cover any kicks. The kicker should still aim to loft the ball as high as possible on a long kick off to give chasers an opportunity to exert immediate pressure on the opposition and force

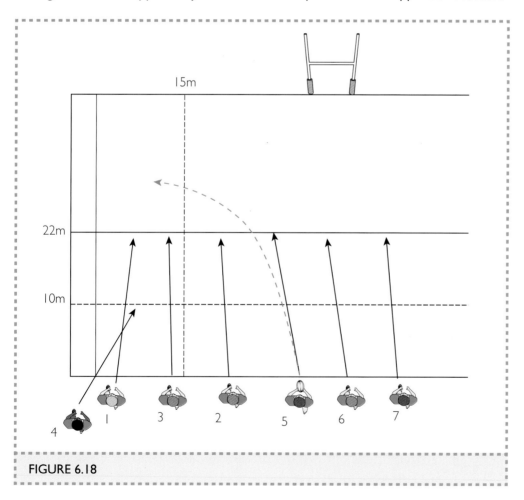

FIGURE 6.18

them into contact. Often, teams chasing long kick offs have an incongruous tendency to advance more slowly than on short kick offs, even though they have more ground to cover. This gives the opposition more time to plan their attack and clear the ball to space. Players should be encouraged to close down their opposition as early as possible, maintaining the defensive line.

Split kick off

A split kick off spreads resources across the field, which in turn separates the opposition. This presents an opportunity to jump against fewer players, and possibly some with less experience and practice in fielding kick offs.

This set-up provides a range of kick–chase options, from long kick offs to the corners, short kick offs to the left or right, or a short kick off straight ahead. All options have players in position to contest the kick or pressurise their opponents. Whatever choice of kick is made, if

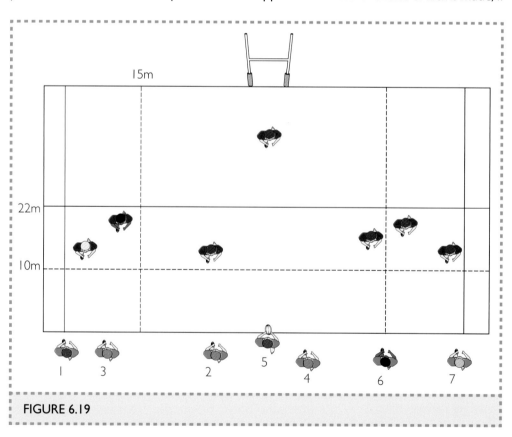

FIGURE 6.19

possession is lost, players on the opposite side to where the ball is kicked should work hard to connect with their teammates and establish the defensive line.

RECEIVING TEAM

The positioning of the receiving team is influenced by the positioning of the opposition and how they are set up to chase their kick off. In most cases, a team will load one side of the field with chasers as this also helps to establish the defensive line quickly if the ball is lost.

Since the ball is in the air longer on longer kicks, there is little need to position more than one player back to cover long kick offs. If the kicker kicks long left, either the receiving fly half (5) or halfback (4) will be able to collect the ball before the opposition. If the kicker kicks long right, either the receiving fly half or wing (7) will have time to collect the ball. Long kick offs present more of an opportunity for a counterattack as the catcher is not under such immediate pressure. Where possible, the ball should be moved quickly to the middle of the

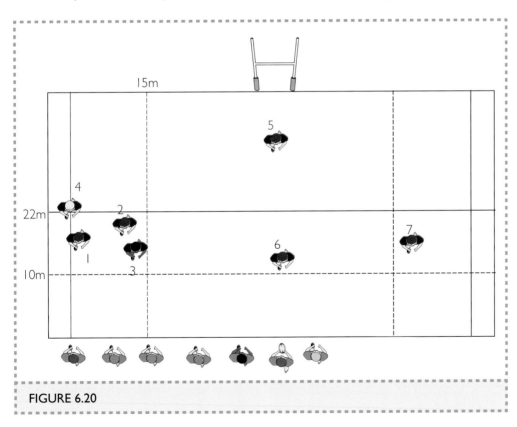

FIGURE 6.20

field, with all players working back to achieve an attacking alignment with sufficient width and depth to stretch the defence and set up the link structure.

The bigger threat is when a kick is lofted high around the 10-metre line. The Props (1 and 3) are the designated catchers, and both have designated support players (4 and 2 respectively). Players should stand a couple of metres back from where they expect the ball to land, so that they can run and jump to catch, keeping the ball and the opposition in vision at all times. The support players aim to lift or at least provide support for their catcher. There is value to being in the air for the catch, as the laws of the game protect you from being tackled until you land. This checks the speed of the chasers and disrupts the timing of their tackle. The support player provides the necessary immediate support on the catch, and adopts the role of first support player if the catcher is tackled to ground.

When the opposition team split and spread across the field, threatening a kick to either side, the receiving team should aim for maximum coverage of the field.

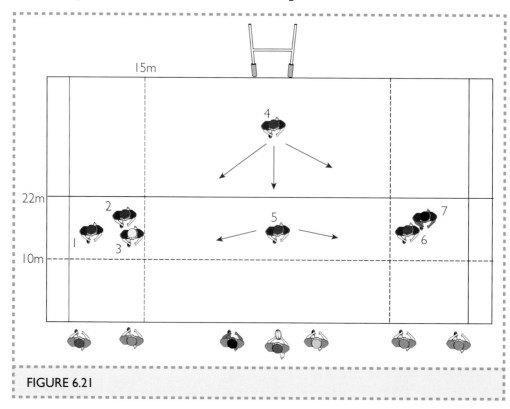

FIGURE 6.21

In this situation, the receiving team is able to retrieve long kick offs in the same way, with one player back. To cover the opposition on short kick offs, the receiving team has to modify its formation, spread resources and anticipate threats. The principles are the same – of aiming to provide support to catchers both in the air and on the ground.

22-metre drop-outs

22-metre drop-outs happen far less frequently in sevens than in fifteens, but teams should still have a system to retain the ball. As soon as the ball is touched down behind the try line, players should move with urgency to the 22-metre line to be in position to take a quick drop-out. The ball should be given to a player with no defender in front of him, who aims to take the kick before the defence has time to organise itself. The kicker's first priority is always to take a little drop-kick to himself, staying low over the ball to maximise control. It is useful

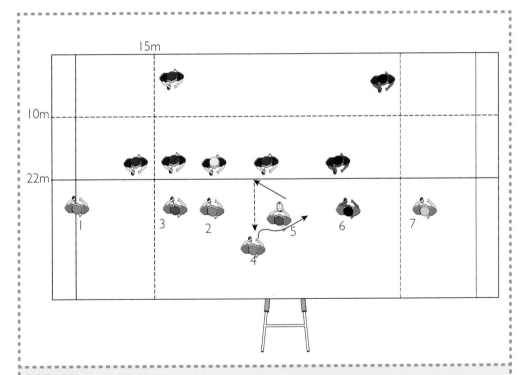

FIGURE 6.22

In this situation, it is the halfback who stands in a deeper position directly behind the kicker to receive the pass.

for all players in the team to be able to execute this type of kick. Support players must then react quickly to give the ball carrier an immediate option to pass away from pressure.

The kicker can still take a short kick to himself even if the defence is well-organised and has covered an attempt to take the kick quickly. The execution is simple; the kicker stays very low over his drop-kick, and instantly throws the ball back through his legs to a support player, to avoid a tackle contest and retain possession.

Another option is to kick long down the 15-metre channels with an organised defensive line in pursuit. This may surrender possession, but a good chase can exert considerable pressure on the opposition. It is imperative that the chasing team maintains a connected defensive line and aims to advance quicker than their opponents can retreat.

The priority when *receiving* a 22-metre drop-out is to position to prevent the opposition from taking the drop-kick quickly, and give the defence more time to organise. Five players should spread across the 22-metre line to cover the short kick, with two players deep in sweeping roles to cover the long kick. When the ball is caught, players should quickly form into an attacking unit, support in threes, and work to set up the link structure.

LESSON 6: INVEST IN PRIMARY POSSESSION

Checklist

- ☐ The scrum and scrum starters
- ☐ The lineout and lineout starters
- ☐ Free-kicks and set plays
- ☐ Short, long and split kick offs
- ☐ Kick off receipt
- ☐ 22-metre drop-outs

7 CONTROL THE TEMPO

Players should develop an understanding of controlling the tempo of a game, and distinguish between opportunities to play *fast* and times to play *steady*.

Playing fast is when the attack moves the ball to players whose aim is to strike at the defence and beat their opponents within that phase of play. Playing steady is when attackers deliberately slow the attack, to set up a change of pace to beat the defence. Playing with tempo in this way does not allow the defence to achieve rhythm in its play, and generally keeps it guessing.

The attack should always play fast off every set piece, and try to play fast off every ruck wherever possible. Attackers playing fast should look to move the ball into space before defenders can cover, or use the attacking movement patterns to strike at the defence. Playing fast gets you to the try line sooner!

The attack should only play steady when the ball is in the middle of the field, when all attackers are on their feet, and when there is a rough balance of players either side, as there is in the link structure. The player who slows down the attack to play steady retreats as he decelerates, giving time for the attack to consolidate and scan for options. Specifically, the attackers are looking for *numbers*. When the attack is playing seven players against six, there is always an overlap somewhere; sometimes it can take a steadying of the attack for this overlap to be exposed.

When *steady* is called, support players should aim to quickly achieve depth and width in their alignment, ready for the ball carrier to move the ball or initiate an attack. It is the responsibility of the support players to send information to the ball carrier and communicate where the overlap exists. The ball carrier then moves the ball accordingly. Where the defence has equal numbers, the ball carrier should seize the initiative, call an attacking movement pattern with the support players on either side of him, and then explosively change the pace of the attack. It is this acceleration that is the essence of playing steady, and not the initial slowing down. The slowing down is just a means to set up a dynamic change of pace in the attack, and to actually play faster!

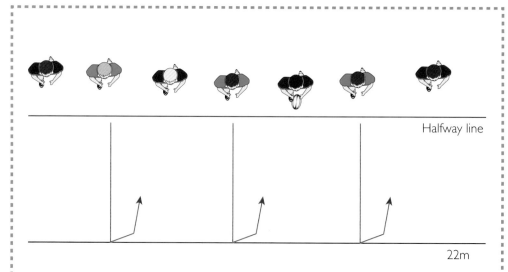

- The same set-up can be used for a 3 v 2, 4 v 3, 5 v 4, 6 v 5, 7 v 6.
- The attackers play the ball when defenders reach the 10m line and turn to defend.
- The drill continues for a set number of phases, or until the attack score. The more players in the drill, the more phases they are allowed to try to score.

FIGURE 7.1 3 v 2 / 4 v 3 / 5 v 4 / 6 v 5 / 7 v 6 Numbers Attack-Defence

A steady must not be played out wide, as attacking options are more limited and the defence can close down the attack easily. Where the steady invites a hard press from the defence, the attack should retain control, and either play with urgency to the detected overlap or use an attacking movement pattern to exploit the commitment and movement of the defenders.

A steady should not be confused with the situation when the ball carrier just hesitates and freezes in attack. This is often the result of a lack of both conviction from the ball carrier and communication from support, and nothing to do with the deliberate action and call to play 'steady'.

The concept of 'pulling out' in attack may also be wrongly confused with playing steady. The traditional concept of support involves players passing and then immediately falling back to a deep position to receive the ball – apparently providing an option for the ball carrier to *pull out* of the attack. This style of support play exerts little pressure on the opposition, and will ultimately fail against structured defences that are connected and quick to advance. Furthermore, the action of immediately dropping back after a pass also leaves the receiver with limited direct attacking options around him, and defies the principle of going forward.

Go forward is still the number one principle of the game of rugby – sevens or fifteens: if you don't go forward, you simply don't score. An attack that does not engage with the principle of *go forward* will be tackled behind the gain line,[11] giving the defence the opportunity to hit contact with momentum, and counter-ruck with force. There is no longer a place in the game for *pulling out* in attack.

Playing fast is undoubtedly the best way to play sevens, and players should be encouraged to acknowledge the attacking movement patterns as the key tools for quick and spontaneous attacking play. The reality is that attackers will need the *steady* call at times to consolidate, recharge and reload, ready to strike again. The ideal is that players have the awareness and fitness to play fast and aim to break the defence with every phase of attack, where a tackle simply sets a platform to play fast again.

[11] The gain line, also termed 'advantage line', is an imaginary line that runs through a tackle, ruck or set piece, that can be used to measure if an attacking team has gone forward.

LESSON 7: CONTROL THE TEMPO

Checklist

☐ Play fast

☐ Steady attack

8

COACH THROUGH THE GAME

Nothing teaches the game of sevens better than the game itself. The aim in a sevens coaching programme is to start playing games as quickly and as often as possible – not necessarily full contact games; just gameplay. Coaching through games offers the best learning platform for players, and maximises both participation and understanding.

You certainly do not start the coaching programme by teaching players how to pass further, even though this is a core skill requirement of the game. You start with team structures, in both attack and defence, so that players have a clear idea of what they are working towards. You give them the big picture, and then work on the detail. This is what accelerates understanding and gameplay in a coaching programme.

Sevens is an invasion game, with attackers and defenders. Activities should, therefore, be opposed and competitive wherever possible. In designing simple handling drills, it is still valuable to include an element of pressure, ideally with live defenders, or at least with a limit or challenge of time and space. It is also important to note that whenever you are working on attack, you should also be working on defence, and vice versa. A 2 v 2 drill in attack is also 2 v 2 in defence – don't ignore the opportunity to reinforce good habits in every practice, and always consider both sides of the grid.

The coach can control and dictate the intensity of the activities. Each drill or game practice below has a rating that is a reflection of its technical difficulty level and intensity based on heart rate and GPS tracking data. Short intensive blocks of fitness should be delivered around these technical activities, not just to improve fitness levels but also to challenge players to perform skills and demonstrate understanding under fatigue. These blocks of fitness, and general conditioning ideas for sevens, are available at

www.coachingrugbysevens.com

The coaching programme: from zero to 7 v 7 in seven sessions!				
Session 1				
	Activities	**Ideas covered**		
1	Team reload	☐ Width	☐ Link structure	
2	7 v 5 Attack–defence	☐ Link structure	☐ Numbering up	
		☐ Numbers and equals	☐ Inside cover	
Session 2				
	Activities	**Ideas covered**		
1	Moving defensive line	☐ Numbering up	☐ Inside cover	
		☐ Tracking		
2	2 v 2 Attack–defence	☐ Attacking movement patterns	☐ Switch defence	
		☐ Tracking		
3	7 v 5 Attack–defence	☐ Link structure	☐ Inside cover	
		☐ Numbering up		
Session 3				
	Activities	**Ideas covered**		
1	1 v 3 Track defence	☐ Tracking	☐ Individual technique	
		☐ Inside cover		

2	3 v 3 Attack–defence	☐ Support in threes ☐ Attacking movement patterns ☐ Numbering up	☐ Inside cover ☐ Individual technique ☐ Counter-ruck
3	7 v 6 Attack–defence	☐ Link structure ☐ Numbers and equals ☐ Attacking movement patterns ☐ Support in threes	☐ Numbering up ☐ Inside cover ☐ Post-tackle work rate

Session 4

	Activities	Ideas covered	
1	1 v 1 Various	☐ Tracking ☐ Individual technique	☐ Counter-ruck
2	Moving 2 v 2 attack–defence	☐ Attacking movement patterns ☐ Tracking	☐ Switch defence
3	7 v 7 Attack–defence	☐ Restarts ☐ Link structure ☐ Attacking movement patterns ☐ Support in threes	☐ Post-tackle work rate ☐ Numbering up ☐ Inside cover ☐ Tracking
4	3 v 3	☐ Numbers and equals ☐ Support in threes ☐ Attacking movement patterns ☐ Secondary support plays	☐ Numbering up ☐ Inside cover ☐ Individual technique

Session 5

	Activities	Ideas covered	
1	1 v 1 Track defence	☐ Situational analysis ☐ Tracking	☐ Individual technique
2	5 v 4 Steady attack–defence	☐ Control tempo ☐ Numbers and equals ☐ Attacking movement patterns ☐ Support in threes	☐ Numbering up ☐ Inside cover ☐ Tracking ☐ Post-tackle work rate

| 3 | 7 v 7 Attack–defence | ☐ Situational analysis ☐ Advanced link structure ☐ Numbers and equals ☐ Attacking movement patterns ☐ Secondary support plays | ☐ Support in threes ☐ Numbering up ☐ Inside cover ☐ Tracking ☐ Post-tackle work rate |

Session 6

	Activities	Ideas covered	
1	Team reload	☐ Width	☐ Link structure
2	1 v 1 + 1 Ruck attack–defence	☐ Numbers and equals ☐ Numbering up	☐ Inside cover ☐ Individual technique
3	7 v 7 Attack–defence	☐ Set piece and starters ☐ Link structure ☐ Numbers and equals ☐ Support in threes ☐ Attacking movement patterns ☐ Secondary support plays	☐ Set piece defence ☐ Numbering up ☐ Inside cover ☐ Individual technique ☐ Post-tackle work rate

Session 7

	Activities	Ideas covered	
1	1 + 1 v 1 Attack–defence	☐ Tracking	☐ Individual technique
2	2 v 3 Attack–defence	☐ Attacking movement patterns ☐ Tracking	☐ Inside cover ☐ Switch defence
3	7 v 7 Attack–defence	☐ Free kicks ☐ Link structure ☐ Numbers and equals ☐ Support in threes ☐ Attacking movement patterns	☐ Secondary support plays ☐ Numbering up ☐ Inside cover ☐ Individual technique ☐ Post-tackle work rate

Glossary of practical activities

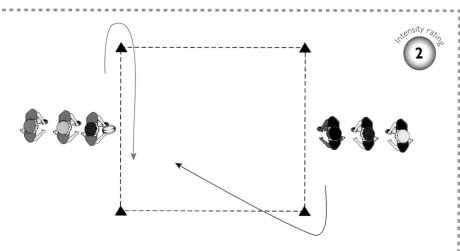

- Players line up on either side of a grid. On one side attackers, the other defenders.
- The ball carrier chooses which marker to run around, and the defender goes around the marker at the opposite end of the grid.
- The defender aims to track and tackle the ball carrier and prevent a score.
- Whether or not a try is scored, the defender joins the attackers line and vice versa.
- Extension activity is 1 + 1 v 1 + 1 — attacker has support for offload, defender has inside cover.

FIGURE 8.1 1 v 1 Attack–defence

Intensity rating

2

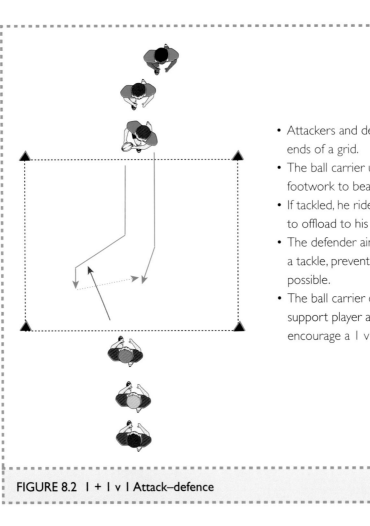

- Attackers and defenders on opposite ends of a grid.
- The ball carrier uses speed and footwork to beat his opponent.
- If tackled, he rides the tackle and aims to offload to his support player.
- The defender aims to track and effect a tackle, preventing the offload if possible.
- The ball carrier can only use the support player after contact, to encourage a 1 v 1 and offload.

FIGURE 8.2 1 + 1 v 1 Attack–defence

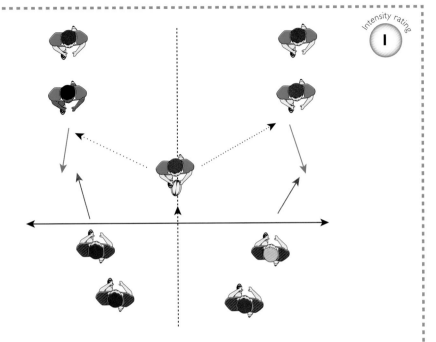

Intensity rating

1

- A halfback passes both left and right to start the drill.
- The defender nominates, tracks and tackles the first receiver.
- The attacker runs forward and checks to see if his opponent has over-tracked.
- The drill can also be practice for the halfback running off the ruck.

FIGURE 8.3 1 v 1 Track defence

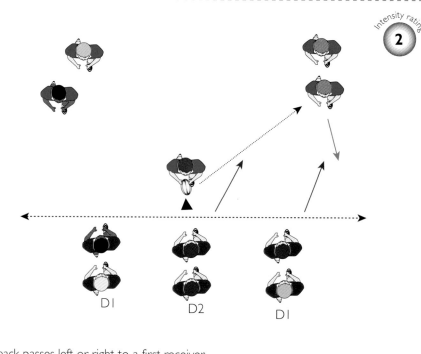

Intensity rating

2

- A halfback passes left or right to a first receiver.
- The defender (D1) marking the first receiver talks, tracks and tackles.
- The first receiver runs and checks if his opponent has overtracked.
- The defender behind the ruck (D2) covers the inside of the defender D1.
- More attackers and defenders can be added to the drill.
- The drill can also be practice for the halfback running off the ruck.

FIGURE 8.4 1 v 1 + 1 Ruck attack–defence

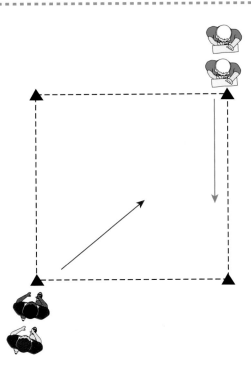

- The skill level of players determines the size of the grid; better players need a bigger grid.
- Players with tackle shields on one corner; tacklers on the diagonally opposite corner.
- Shield carriers simulate ball carriers and runs straight.
- Defender track, talk and tackle.
- Timed drill; after a set time, players change sides of the drill.
- Players then swap roles.

FIGURE 8.5 Individual tackle technique

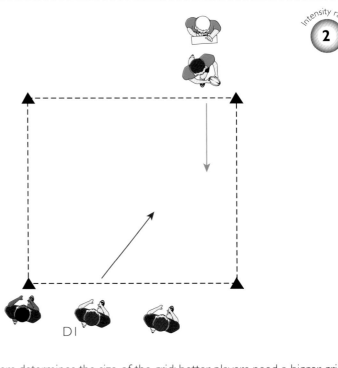

- The skill level of players determines the size of the grid; better players need a bigger grid.
- Attackers work in pairs – ball carrier and tackle shield carrier, who simulates an arriving first support player.
- Defenders work in threes – with tackler and inside and outside support.
- Central defender (D1) talks, tracks and tackles the ball carrier.
- Either the inside or outside support defender counter rucks against the shield carrier, depending on the angle of attack.

FIGURE 8.6 1 + 1 v 1 + 1 Counter-ruck technique

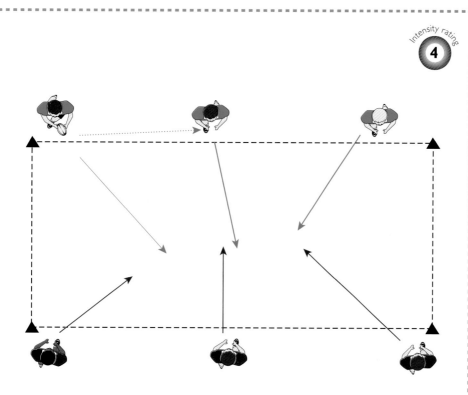

Intensity rating
4

- 3 v 3; players face each other across a grid.
- Both attackers and defenders must start in a position covering the full width of the grid.
- The width and depth of the grid can be adjusted to target different objectives.
- The attackers pass the ball between them, until one decides to attack.
- The ball carrier aims to evade the tacklers and get in behind the defence to facilitate ruck efficiency.
- Both teams aim to win the tackle contest.

FIGURE 8.7 3 v 3 Support in 3s

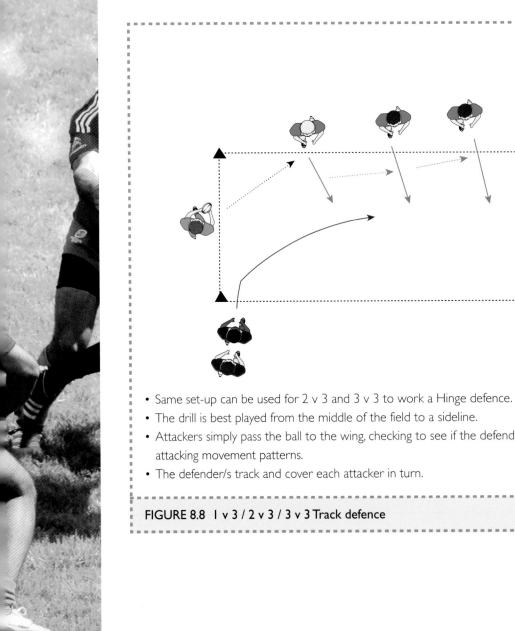

Intensity rating
4

- Same set-up can be used for 2 v 3 and 3 v 3 to work a Hinge defence.
- The drill is best played from the middle of the field to a sideline.
- Attackers simply pass the ball to the wing, checking to see if the defender/s over-track. No attacking movement patterns.
- The defender/s track and cover each attacker in turn.

FIGURE 8.8   1 v 3 / 2 v 3 / 3 v 3 Track defence

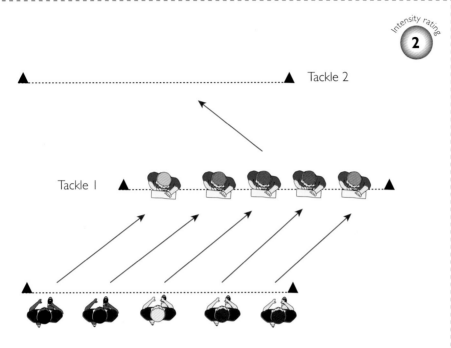

Intensity rating
2

Tackle 2

Tackle 1

- 5 defenders form a defensive line between 2 cones
- 5 shield carriers line up opposite them.
- The defenders number up from the outside, identify their opponent, and hit the correct shield to simulate a tackle.
- After the tackle, the defenders perform a set number of press-ups (e.g. 3), while shield carriers reposition for Tackle 2.
- Defenders again slide across field to hit their pad.

FIGURE 8.9 Moving defensive line

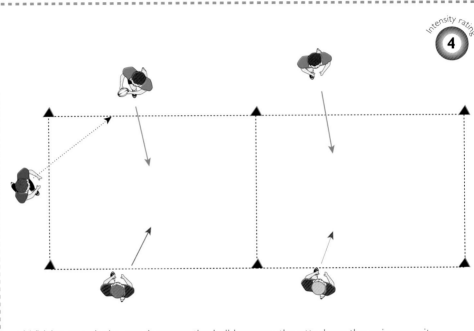

Intensity rating 4

- Whichever pair the coach passes the ball become the attackers; the pair opposite defends.
- The attackers try to beat the defence with the attacking movement patterns.
- There is no limit on width.

FIGURE 8.10 2 v 2 Attack–defence

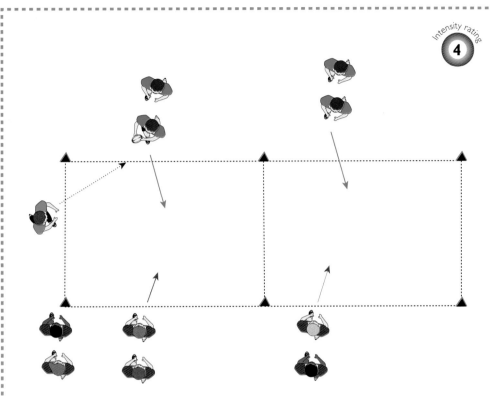

Intensity rating
4

- The drill is set up and run the same as 2 v 2.
- There are three defenders; the third is just to provide inside cover and is not marking a specific attacker.

FIGURE 8.11 2 v 3 Attack–defence

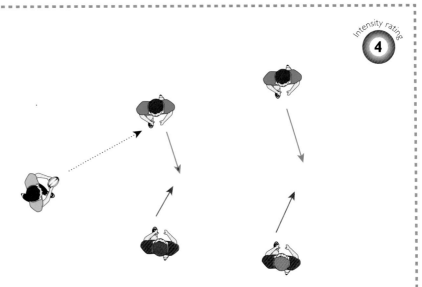

Intensity rating

4

- There are no cones to mark the drill; players are just instructed to stand opposite each other for a 2 v 2, as illustrated.
- The coach runs in random directions, and players have to keep their alignment.
- Whichever pair the coach passes to is the attacking team.
- Once the coach passes the ball, the drill becomes a simple 2 v 2 practice.

FIGURE 8.12 Moving 2 v 2 attack–defence

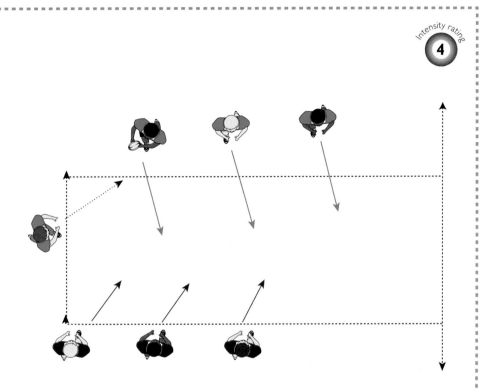

Intensity rating

4

- Players in threes at opposite ends of a wide grid.
- The drill is best played from the middle of the field to a sideline.
- The attackers try to beat the defence with the attacking movement patterns and secondary support plays.
- The defence number up and use inside cover to prevent a try.

FIGURE 8.13 3 v 3 Attack–defence

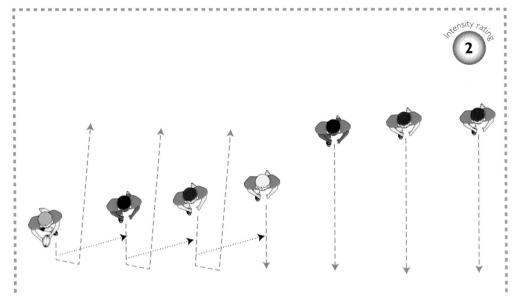

Intensity rating

2

- 5 or more players spread across the full width of the field, running from try line to try line.
- The players pass the ball along the line, reloading after their pass.
- Players pass from wing to wing, but can test the reload of inside players by changing the direction of the passing.
- Though unopposed, this is a great drill for developing wide passing and good habits in alignment and reload.

FIGURE 8.14 Team reload

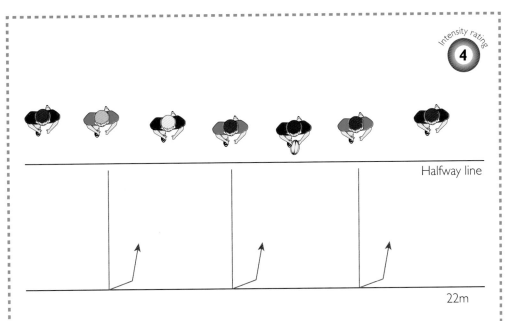

Intensity rating
4

Halfway line

22m

- The same set-up can be used for a 3 v 2, 4 v 3, 5 v 4, 6 v 5, 7 v 6.
- The attackers play the ball when defenders reach the 10m line and turn to defend.
- The drill continues for a set number of phases, or until the attack score. The more players in the drill, the more phases they are allowed to try to score.

FIGURE 8.15 3 v 2 / 4 v 3 / 5 v 4 / 6 v 5 / 7 v 6 Numbers attack–defence

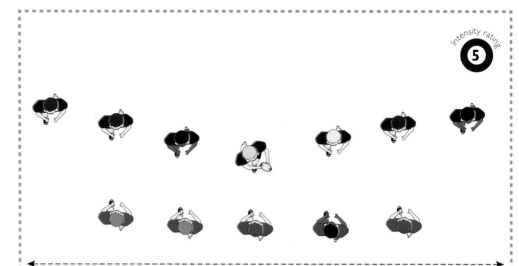

Intensity rating

5

22m line

- The same set-up can be used for a 7 v 6; always using the full width of the field.
- The defenders start on the 22m line; the attack aim to score on the try line.
- The drill continues for a set period of time, after which the players change roles.

FIGURE 8.16 7 v 4 / 7 v 5 / 7 v 6 Attack–defence

LESSON 8: PLAY THE GAME

Checklist

Attack:

- [ ] Link structure
- [ ] Attacking movement patterns
- [ ] Support in threes
- [ ] Numbers and equals
- [ ] Restarts
- [ ] Situational analysis
- [ ] Advanced link structure
- [ ] Set piece and starters
- [ ] Secondary support plays
- [ ] Control tempo
- [ ] Free kicks

Defence:

- [ ] Numbering up
- [ ] Inside cover
- [ ] Tracking
- [ ] Individual tackle technique
- [ ] Counter-ruck
- [ ] Switch defence
- [ ] Post-tackle work rate
- [ ] Restart receipt
- [ ] Set piece defence

9 KEEP LEARNING

Many of the lessons we have learnt in sevens can be applied to fifteens, in order to give our attacking play in fifteens the same purpose and potency as in sevens.

Like sevens, fifteens can also be interpreted as a numbers game; where the key to attack is playing in a clear structure that allows the attacking team to manipulate defenders, and develop attacking movement patterns to exploit how we *know* defenders will position and move.

Finding an overlap in fifteens, for example, is far more difficult than it is in sevens. Most often, the defence will at least equate numbers with the attack, and in some cases have more numbers in their defensive line than in the attacking line, depending on how many players the attack commits to contact. Like in sevens, the attacking team must aim to be efficient in its use of support players in contact, to deny the defensive team a numerical advantage in alignment. For example, if the attack commits six players to contact, and the defence only commits two, the attack is clearly short of numbers in the attacking line.

The goal is to create one-on-ones, so it is clear to an attacker who is marking him, whom to beat and where space will be created. To set up one-on-ones, the attacking alignment needs to force a spread alignment in the defence, to expand the space between defenders, exposing and isolating them for attack. The defence will spread if there are attacking threats to cover, so the aim of the attack is to ensure that there are enough threats, positioned appropriately and coordinated ready to strike.

Packing fifteen players into a defence is always going to seriously affect the space available to attack. Even fitting fifteen players into the *attacking* team can cause organisational problems on the field, so it is again necessary to simplify the equation, and divide the attacking team into smaller and more manageable units. In sevens, the *link structure* is used as a framework for attack, setting width in alignment and ensuring efficiency of support.

A similar structure is possible in fifteens. Instead of two attacking units of three players, in fifteens the team should be divided into three units of four players, with the remaining three players assigned to the role of linking the attacking units together. The three *link* players are playmakers that manage and make decisions on the direction of play; the attacking units are the firepower across the full width of the field, which forces the necessary spread alignment in the defence.

In the fifteens framework, the attacking team operates in three broad channels on the field, with each unit occupying one channel. After an attack in their channel of the field, each attacking unit reloads into the same channel ready to attack again. Just like in the sevens link structure, the attacking units move on the field like pistons of an engine – moving forwards to strike, and back to reload, keeping to a designated channel of the field.

The three link players – usually 9, 10 and 15 – interchange to ensure that the ball is cleared quickly from the attacking unit in contact, and that the two remaining units are always connected to the attack. This retains a spread defensive alignment and keeps the pressure on the defence.

The three-channel system notably facilitates and optimises attack from 'mid rucks' and 'wide rucks'. Both can be easily constructed within the game, and just as easily replicated for development and repetition in training. Attacking movement patterns should be designed specifically for attack from a mid ruck or a wide ruck.

Mid rucks

A mid ruck (that is a ruck in the middle channel) is a prolific attacking platform because it creates a 'split field', turning 15 vs 15 into a much simpler equation. When the defending team commits two players to a mid ruck, the attacking team is faced with a beatable defensive line of just five or six players, either side of the ruck. And if the defending team commits more than two players to the tackle, the odds increase further in favour of the attacking team.

Four players running off a playmaker provides numerous options in terms of the shape of their alignment and potential attacking movement patterns. The extra numbers in fifteens offer valuable depth of support that is missing in sevens, and which facilitates a greater range of running lines and options. The priority should be to cut off the fringe ruck defenders from the defensive line, leaving the wider defenders isolated and vulnerable

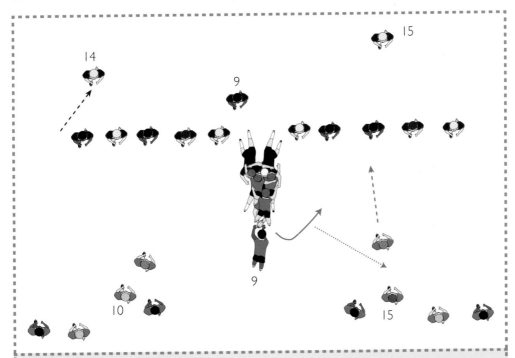

FIGURE 9.1 Mid ruck attack
The scrum half plays as one of the link players, while the other link players (usually 10 & 15) position as playmakers connected to the attacking units on either side of the ruck.

to attack. This can be achieved with the scrum half combining simply with a runner (as illustrated). When executed effectively, a mid ruck exposes three or four defenders who are left to cover one half of the field, which is a favourable situation for a well-drilled attacking unit running well-rehearsed attacking movement patterns.

Wide rucks

A wide ruck is a weaker attacking platform, just as it is in sevens, because the defence only has to defend one side of the ruck and can advance with speed and confidence.

From an attack in a wide channel, one *link* plays halfback, a second plays first receiver to the unit in the middle of the field, and the third plays in a deep wider role to form a link to the unit on the other side of the field.

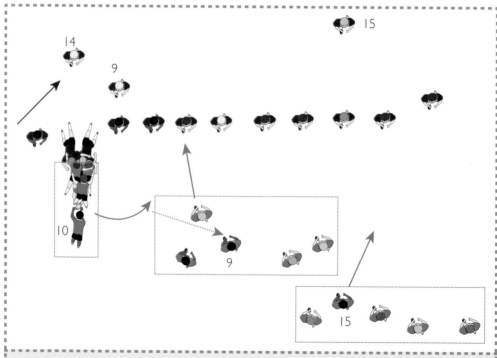

FIGURE 9.2 Wide ruck attack
While one unit is in contact, the other two units reload ready to attack, with the link players connecting one side of the field to the other.

possible to maintain forward momentum and set up another mid ruck. The option to link from one wide channel to the other is also essential to keep the defensive line spread and vulnerable to breaks.

Just like in sevens, this three-unit, three-channel structure ensures that there is an efficient and ready support unit around the ball carrier at all times. This accelerates the reaction speed of support players to contact, giving the attacking team an edge in ball security and continuity. In sevens, the attacking units are fluid, with players having to frequently regenerate a support unit of three, especially when the link player is caught in contact; but in fifteens, the attacking units stay fixed, with players supporting exclusively within their unit, and keeping to their channel of the field.

The final task is to decide which players to assign to which attacking unit; what roles they play within that unit; and how they get into their channels from structured possessions such as scrums and lineouts, and less structured possessions like kick receipts and turnovers. There are actually not many variables to consider; the key is to find an efficient way of moving into the structure from any source of possession, with as consistent a method as possible.

This is just a sample of how thinking in sevens can influence the way we coach and consider the fifteen-a-side game. It presents a framework that invites more detail and sets a springboard for further innovation on the game. The ideas are easy to adapt and advance; the team could be divided differently; there could be more link players, or none at all; alignment could take on new shapes; the field could evolve into more channels or fewer; and attacking units could *flash* and *fold* and move more fluidly around the field. For this detail, and for more new thinking on sevens *and* fifteens, head to Lesson 10!

10 STAY CONNECTED

For more information or assistance on anything included in this book, to share your own ideas or just to keep up-to-date with how the game advances, stay in touch at:

marcus@coachingrugbysevens.com

ACKNOWLEDGEMENTS

Thanks to all of the people and places who have given me the opportunity to learn in and through the game, now seven years on from the first edition of this book. Thanks especially to Brian O'Shea for his time in reviewing and discussing the second edition, and for his overall professional mentorship in all things rugby. Thanks to Wade Kelly for being so generous with his technical expertise, making every meeting and training session real professional development. Thanks to Dr Ilan Kogus for his teachings on team leadership and culture that have made the game – and life – so much more enjoyable. Thanks to all of the organisations to date who have given me the opportunity to discover, develop and drive the ideas in this book – most notably to the Singapore Rugby Union, Raffles Institution, The Scots College and Randwick Rugby Club – and to the Rugby Football Union and Australian Rugby Union for the opportunity to present my ideas within their national coach education pathways. Most of all, thanks to my best friend, Tara Blackburn, for always being so supportive of my 'projects⬛, especially this one! There will be more.

Picture credits

Photos on pages 4–5, 8, 10, 14, 22, 58, 84, 97, 120 and 126 © Pavel L Photo and Video/ Shutterstock.com; page 49 © AFP/Getty Images; pages 6, 68, 91 and 118 © Kin Cheung/AP/ Press Association Images; pages 18, 42, 148 and 154 © Julie Jacobson/AP/Press Association Images; page 21 © Adam Davy/EMPICS Sport; page 94 © Craig Halkett/PA Archive/Press Association Images; page 123 © Shizuo Kambayashi/AP/Press Association Images; and page 125 © Kamran Jebreili/AP/Press Association Images.

INDEX